Spelling Success

CLASS 6

Peter Clutterbuck

Blake
EDUCATION
Better ways to learn

To Jessie O'Brien

Spelling Success Class 6

Published by Scholastic India Pvt. Ltd.
A-27, Ground Floor, Sigma Centre
Infocity-1, Sector 34, Gurgaon-122001 (India)
Info-in@scholastic.asia

Author: Peter Clutterbuck
Editor: Kerry Davies
Cover and internal design: Janice Bowles
Typesetter: Julian Mole, Post Pre Press.

ISBN: 978-93-5471-904-2
First edition 2010
This reprint edition: June 2024
Printed in India

Contents

Term 1

✓ Tick when completed

Term 2

✓ Tick when completed

Contents continued

Term 3

✓ Tick when completed

Term 4

✓ Tick when completed

Appendixes

About This Book

The *Spelling Success* series provides students with learning activities that embrace the different elements of the spelling system. Each book focuses on the different scope and sequences in the development of spelling skills for each age group or skill level.

These books are not a complete spelling course in themselves, neither are they meant to be, but they provide both students and teachers with the content needed to produce best practices in spelling.

The activities in each book are sequential through the four terms of the school year. This means that it's best to start at the beginning of the Term 1 section and work though to the end, before commencing Term 2 activities, and so on. There are 76 units in this book, 18 per term plus four Review and Test units. Each term is divided into the four areas of knowledge that need to be understood and learned in order to develop a comprehensive mastery of spelling:

Phonological Knowledge — how words sound

Word Function Knowledge — how word function can change spelling

Meaning Knowledge — how context can change word form

Word History Knowledge — how words have been derived

The Phonological Knowledge and the Word Function Knowledge sections include Revision and Test sheets for each term. Four units of Review and Test sheets covering the whole book are provided at the end of Term 4.

This book also contains useful tools to support students with their spelling. At the back of the book you'll find:

- ★ Useful Words list
- ★ WINK: Words I Need to Know — space to record problematic words
- ★ Some Tips for Learning to Spell
- ★ Assessment checklist
- ★ Glossary of Terms

Answers to all activities are provided in a special liftout section. A useful **topic list** for the whole year is given before the units.

Spelling Success provides an integrated method of teaching phonics, spelling and vocabulary. These books will improve literacy skills through effective instruction and evaluation based on the latest research into how spelling is best taught and learned successfully.

Book 6 Topic Chart

TOPIC	UNIT
Adding ion or ation to base words	67
Adding ion to base words	48,66
Adding the suffix ary	64
Adding the suffix ion	31
Adding the suffix ly	30
Adjectives and nouns, ance or ant endings	49
Assimilated or absorbed prefixes	65
Change of meaning by stress	71
Complex consonant groups, ch and tch, dge and ge	41
Compound words	52
Consonant groups, ph and gh as an f sound	40
Contractions	35
Doubling, adding ed	46
Doubling, adding ing	47
Final unstressed syllables, ar and or	38
Final unstressed syllables, et and it	37
Final unstressed syllables, il and al	20
Final unstressed syllables, le and el	19
Greek root words	54
Hard and soft c	56
Hard and soft g	55
Homographs	34
Homophones	16,17
Latin root words	36

TOPIC	UNIT
Long a sound patterns	2
Long e sound patterns	4
Long i sound patterns	6
Long o sound patterns	5
Long u sound patterns	3
Number prefixes	72
Old English root words	18
Past tense verbs	28
Plurals, adding s or es	10
Plurals, complete change or none	13
Plurals, words ending in y	11
Plurals, words ending in f or fe	12
Possessives	29
Short a sound patterns	1
Silent letters	39
Sound patterns, au and ou	24
Sound patterns, ea	22
Sound patterns, er	59
Sound patterns, g as a j sound	58
Sound patterns, ir and ur	23
Sound patterns, oi, oy and ei	57
Sound patterns, or and oa	21
Sound patterns, y as a long i sound	60
Syllables	42
Vowel alternations	53,70

UNIT 1

Short a sound patterns

Every vowel can be pronounced as either a short or a long sound. The words **maze** and **relation** use the long a sound. The words **apple** and **ant** use the short a sound.

A Each of the words in the box contains the short a sound. Write the correct word in the sentences that follow the box.

attic	**bandage**	**candle**	**package**	**address**
accident	**avenue**	**canvas**	**tragic**	**baptise**

1. There was a bad _______________ at the crossroads last night.
2. They put a _______________ over his bleeding elbow.
3. In the church they lit a _______________ in her memory.
4. We stored lots of old books in the _______________ of our house.
5. He lives in a broad tree-lined _______________ in our city.
6. It was a _______________ happening that saddened us all.
7. The tent was made of waterproof _______________.
8. His new _______________ is 15 Wattle Street.
9. I had to collect the _______________ from the post office.
10. We have agreed to _______________ the baby in this church.

B Sort the following words into short a and long a sounds.

cattle	**sacred**	**maggot**
agent	**capsule**	**painter**

Short a sound	**Long a sound**
_______________	_______________
_______________	_______________
_______________	_______________

Parent/Teacher Signature   Date

Long a sound patterns

Every vowel is either a short or a long sound. The words **apple** and **ant** are pronounced with the short a sound. The words **maze** and **relation** use the long a sound.

A The words in the box all contain the long a sound pattern. Match each to a word it can be linked to below.

cradle	**raven**	**nation**	**baseball**	**subway**	**vacant**
raisin	**decay**	**crayon**	**mistake**	**pavement**	**bacon**

1. tooth ____________
2. bird ____________
3. bun ____________
4. football ____________
5. pencil ____________
6. pork ____________
7. Australia ____________
8. footpath ____________
9. baby ____________
10. error ____________
11. train ____________
12. full ____________

B Sort the following words into short a and long a sound patterns.

dismay	**traffic**	**basement**	**grateful**	**napkin**	**vapour**
hammer	**debate**	**pattern**	**gallop**	**waiter**	**plastic**

Short a sound

____________ ____________

____________ ____________

____________ ____________

Long a sound

____________ ____________

____________ ____________

____________ ____________

Parent/Teacher Signature Date

Long and short e sound patterns

Vowels are either a short or a long sound. The words **peck** and **letter** are pronounced with the short e sound. The words **these** and **tree** use the long e sound.

A The words in the box have the long e sound pattern. In some the accent is on the first syllable, while the accent is on the second syllable in others. Choose a word from the box to match each meaning below.

fever	**eager**	**cheetah**	**steeple**	**canteen**
beaver	**beetle**	**conceal**	**delete**	**compete**

1. a kind of small insect ____________
2. to rival or go against ____________
3. a creature that builds dams across rivers ____________
4. a very fast spotted cat ____________
5. illness with a high temperature ____________
6. part of a church ____________
7. to leave out or omit ____________
8. place that serves food ____________
9. keen or willing ____________
10. hide ____________

B Look closely at the words in the box. Write them under their headings below.

trapeze	**denim**	**breezy**	**agree**	**breathe**	**feather**
metal	**free**	**lemon**	**pedal**	**credit**	**appeal**

Short e sound		**Long e sound**	
____________	____________	____________	____________
____________	____________	____________	____________
____________	____________	____________	____________

Parent/Teacher Signature Date

UNIT 4

Long and short i sound patterns

Vowels are either a short or a long sound. The words **pick** and **written** are pronounced with the short i sound. The words **five** and **knife** use the long i sound.

A The following words contain the long i sound pattern. In some the accent falls on the first syllable, while in others it is on the second syllable. Each one can be linked in some way to a word below. Write each word beside its link word.

polite	**nightmare**	**lightning**	**bridle**	**sinus**	**spider**
reptile	**quiet**	**frighten**	**iceberg**	**rival**	**sightseer**

1. ____________ web
2. ____________ saddle
3. ____________ dream
4. ____________ rude
5. ____________ opponent
6. ____________ Antarctica
7. ____________ nose
8. ____________ thunder
9. ____________ lizard
10. ____________ tourist
11. ____________ scare
12. ____________ noisy

B The box contains words with either the long i sound or the short i sound. Write the words under their headings below.

skinny	**wildlife**	**minus**	**picture**	**blizzard**	**ninety**
describe	**ribbon**	**river**	**visor**	**siren**	**signal**

Short i sound

____________ ____________

____________ ____________

____________ ____________

Long i sound

____________ ____________

____________ ____________

____________ ____________

Parent/Teacher Signature Date

Long and short o sound patterns

Vowel are pronounced as either a short or a long sound.
The words **dock** and **rotten** use the short o sound.
The words **hose** and **hotel** use the long o sound.

A The following words contain the long o sound pattern. In some the accent is on the first syllable, while the accent is on the second syllable in others. Choose a word from the box to complete each sentence.

donate	**lonely**	**telescope**	**violent**	**broken**
robot	**postage**	**explode**	**propose**	**enclose**

1. We waited anxiously for the bomb to ________________ .
2. The ________________ on the parcel will cost five dollars.
3. In this factory one ________________ does the work of ten people.
4. Being a lighthouse keeper was a ________________ life last century.
5. The explorers studied the nearby land through a ________________ .
6. We were not sure what he wanted to ________________ .
7. A ________________ storm rocked the city.
8. The ________________ toy was left in the playground.
9. The wealthy person will ________________ his collection to the museum.
10. I hope you will ________________ some money for me in your next letter.

B The following words contain the long o sound or the short o sound. Write each word under the headings below.

alone	**bottle**	**almost**	**hobby**	**mower**	**comma**
comet	**snowfall**	**nozzle**	**local**	**monster**	**token**

Short o sound		**Long o sound**	
________________	________________	________________	________________
________________	________________	________________	________________
________________	________________	________________	________________

Parent/Teacher Signature Date

Long and short u sound patterns

Vowels are pronounced as either a short or a long sound. The words **duck** and **cluster** have the short **u** sound. The words **duke** and **student** use the long **u** sound.

A The words in the box all use the long **u** sound. Each one can be linked in some way to a word below. Write each word beside its link word.

pupil	**value**	**population**	**tune**	**puncture**	**avenue**
cure	**rescue**	**furniture**	**bugle**	**future**	**refute**

1.save ____________ 7. instrument ____________

2.song ____________ 8. people ____________

3.eye ____________ 9. table, chair ____________

4.street ____________ 10. cost ____________

5.deny ____________ 11. medicine ____________

6.tyre ____________ 12. past ____________

B Sort the following words into short **u** and long **u** sound patterns.

custard	**product**	**avenue**	**lumping**	**confuse**	**crust**
rescue	**statue**	**mustard**	**introduce**	**plum**	**perfume**

Short u sound

____________ ____________

____________ ____________

____________ ____________

Long u sound

____________ ____________

____________ ____________

____________ ____________

Parent/Teacher Signature Date

Revision

The words written in the brackets after each sentence below have either a long or short vowel sound. Choose the correct word and write it in the space.

1. There was a bad ________________ at the crossroads. (attic, accident)
2. The meat of a pig is called ________________ . (vapour, bacon)
3. I saw the pretty red ________________ growing at the side of the road. (raisin, daisy)
4. The baby is sleeping in its ________________ . (ladle, cradle)
5. We were served our meal by a very efficient ________________ . (tailor, waiter)
6. We rode the ________________ around the paddock. (sofa, pony)
7. The ________________ on the letter is quite dear. (postage, hostage)
8. The ________________ lit up the cloudy sky. (lightning, lightening)
9. My favourite ________________ is reading. (lobby, hobby)
10. There was a ________________ storm last night. (violet, violent)
11. In mathematics ________________ means less. (minus, sinus)
12. A ________________ is an animal that makes dams across rivers. (weaver, beaver)
13. Mike and I began to ________________ against each other. (compete, complete)
14. The doctors are trying to find an effective ________________ for this disease. (cure, pure)
15. The accident was really a very ________________ event. (magic, tragic)
16. The clergyman will ________________ the baby tomorrow. (capsize, baptise)

Parent/Teacher Signature   Date

Test 1

The spelling mistake in each sentence has been underlined. Write the correct spelling for the underlined word in the box.

1	I became <u>lonly</u> living in the city.	1
2	She was <u>chosin</u> to be our leader.	2
3	The ship was close to the gigantic <u>iceburg</u>.	3
4	A snake is a type of <u>reptyle</u>.	4
5	We took great <u>delite</u> in telling her.	5
6	She is now a <u>famus</u> film star.	6
7	We must <u>maintane</u> our protests.	7
8	The clothes are stored in the <u>attick</u> of the house.	8
9	Cows and dogs are <u>mammils</u>.	9
10	A <u>cheeta</u> is a swift runner.	10
11	She is ill with a bad <u>feva</u>.	11
12	We bought the sandwiches at the <u>cantine</u>.	12

Total correct ______ / 12

Parent/Teacher Signature   Date

Test 2

Each sentence has one word that is incorrect.
Write the correct word in the box.

1	You must be careful that the fuel does not ignight.	1
2	The water became frozin last night.	2
3	The baby is sleeping in its cradil.	3
4	The trafick is busy today.	4
5	The rich lady will doneight money to the fair.	5
6	I hope the bomb does not expload.	6
7	The spida was spinning a web.	7
8	We could hear the sound of the bugel.	8
9	The shampooh is in the bathroom.	9
10	The car has a punchure in the front tyre.	10
11	What is your present adress?	11
12	There is a lot of furnichure in the room.	12

Total correct ______
12

Parent/Teacher Signature Date

Plurals, adding s or es

Plural means more than one. Nouns form their plurals in a number of ways:

★ By simply adding s.
Examples: one farm, two farms; one table, six tables; one tree, several trees

★ By adding es to nouns that end in ch, s, sh, ss or x.
Examples: one match, a box of matches; one bus, three buses; one glass, a tray of glasses; one marsh, many marshes; one box, a dozen boxes

★ Most nouns that end in o also add es to become plural.
Example: one potato, six potatoes. However, some simply add s.
Example: one piano, two pianos

In the blanks, write the plural of each noun given in brackets at the end of the sentences.

1. The ship fired six ________________ at the aircraft carrier. (torpedo)
2. Our school has two ________________. (piano)
3. I left the five ________________ on the table. (page)
4. There are many ________________ in this garden. (tree)
5. Jack and Sophie hid behind the ________________. (bush)
6. We have many ________________ in our bathroom. (shampoo)
7. The ranger returned with seven ________________. (fox)
8. In the country they hold lots of ________________. (rodeo)
9. We explored the ________________ in this coastal area. (grotto)
10. Oxygen and nitrogen are both important ________________. (gas)
11. We brought all the ________________ from the office. (chair)
12. There are three ________________ in our street. (church)
13. We bought six ________________ from the fruit shop. (mango)
14. She had three ________________ before she got it right. (guess)
15. My mother has five old battery ________________. (radio)
16. We took lots of ________________ to the picnic. (plate)

Parent/Teacher Signature Date

Plurals, words ending in y

Plural means more than one. Nouns form their plurals in a number of ways:

★ Some nouns that end in **y** before a vowel form their plurals simply by adding **s**. Examples: one day, two days; one chimney, a stack of chimneys

★ For nouns that end in **y** before a consonant, drop the **y**, replace it with an **i** and then add **es**. Example: one country, two countries

Write the plural of each noun given in brackets at the end of the sentences.

1. I left the five ________________ on the bench. (cray)
2. We could hear the many ________________ of help from the trapped miners. (cry)
3. There are many ________________ in the paddock. (donkey)
4. We read about the ________________ made by Captain Cook. (journey)
5. Apart from classes we had lots of ________________ at the school. (duty)
6. This building is seven ________________ high. (storey)
7. Australia administers quite a few ________________ . (territory)
8. Our grade has had lots of birthday ________________ this year. (party)
9. We tasted many ________________ from the restaurant. (delicacy)
10. The glasses were carried on the three ________________. (tray)
11. There were several exotic ________________ at the zoo. (monkey)
12. The band played two ________________ during the afternoon. (medley)
13. We travelled home by using the two ________________. (subway)
14. The six ________________ on all the sheets were correct. (tally)
15. Our class has several different ________________ to use. (dictionary)
16. In early Australia ________________ were a popular vehicle. (buggy)

Parent/Teacher Signature   Date

UNIT 12

Plurals, words ending in f or fe

Plural means more than one. Nouns form their plurals in a number of ways:

★ For most nouns that end in f or fe, you change the f to v and add es. Examples: one leaf, two leaves; one knife, a set of knives

★ However, some simply add s. Examples: one chief, two chiefs; one giraffe, a herd of giraffes

Fill in the blanks to give the correct form of the noun in the brackets at the end of each sentence.

1. There are several dangerous ______________ in this area. (reef)
2. The horse had three of its ______________ shod. (hoof)
3. We read all about the ______________ of different explorers. (life)
4. We had ______________ of wine on the table. (carafe)
5. We removed the ______________ from the wall. (shelf)
6. The incident went against several of her ______________. (belief)
7. The ships are anchored at the two ______________. (wharfs)
8. The prince is said to have had several ______________. (wife)
9. The ______________ of houses were blown off in the storm. (roof)
10. There are lots of coloured ______________ on this tree. (leaf)
11. Both the ______________ survived the long trek. (calf)
12. The ______________ of his shirt were frayed. (cuff)
13. The many ______________ here are used by birds for nesting. (cliff)
14. The fairy tale tells of a girl and five ______________. (elf)
15. There are many ______________ in this zoo. (giraffe)
16. The tribal ______________ met to discuss the proposal. (chief)

Parent/Teacher Signature Date

Plurals, complete change or none

Plural means more than one. Nouns form their plurals in a number of ways:

★ Some nouns make their plurals by completely changing their structure. Example: one mouse, two mice

★ Some nouns have no singular form at all. Example: jeans

★ Some nouns have only one word to indicate both singular and plural. Example: one sheep, a flock of sheep

Add the correct form of the nouns given in the brackets at the end of the sentences.

1. He broke several ______________ in the accident. (tooth)
2. We cut the paper with the ______________. (scissors)
3. Both his ______________ were sore after the walk. (foot)
4. There are many ______________ on this farm. (goose)
5. I used a pair of ______________ to pull out the nails. (pliers)
6. The caterpillar produces many ______________. (larva)
7. We took all the ______________ to the beach. (child)
8. Tom has three pairs of ______________. (trousers)
9. Our teacher wears wire-rimmed ______________. (spectacles)
10. Sally measured the ______________ of the three circles. (radius)
11. We heard lots of ______________ from the audience. (applause)
12. We removed all the ______________ from her hair. (louse)
13. There were a lot of ______________ in the holding yard. (cattle)
14. The tree was covered in several different ______________. (fungus)
15. We caught four ______________ in the river. (trout)
16. The ______________ gathered for lunch every week. (woman)

Parent/Teacher Signature   Date

UNIT 14

Revision

A There are twelve nouns hidden in the grid.
Find them and write each one on the first line below.
On the second line write its plural form.

f	l	y	b	e	r	r	y
t	d	i	a	r	y	w	m
r	p	h	o	t	o	o	o
o	f	l	o	o	d	l	n
l	g	l	a	s	s	f	k
l	s	t	o	r	y	j	e
e	a	t	l	a	s	k	y
y	p	a	t	c	h	y	x

1. ______________ ______________
2. ______________ ______________
3. ______________ ______________
4. ______________ ______________
5. ______________ ______________
6. ______________ ______________
7. ______________ ______________
8. ______________ ______________
9. ______________ ______________
10. ______________ ______________
11. ______________ ______________
12. ______________ ______________

B Circle the correct word in the brackets.

1. The (thieves, thiefs) were soon caught by the police.
2. The rabbits were chased by the three (fox, foxes)
3. There are several (goose, geese) on the farm.
4. All the different (shampoos, shampoo) are in the cupboard.
5. We saw lots of (deers, deer) at the zoo.
6. The farmer cut all the (branchs, branches) off the tree.
7. The leader distributed all the new (diarys, diaries) to the students.
8. There were too many (mosquitoes, mosquitos) at the picnic.
9. The baker asked me if I would deliver all the (loafs, loaves)
10. We took the five (trollies, trolleys) back to the supermarket.

Parent/Teacher Signature   Date

Test 2

The spelling mistakes in these sentences have been circled. Write the correct spelling for each circled word in the box.

1	There are four busses in the garage.	1
2	The teacher read us lots of animal storys.	2
3	We saw the monkies at the zoo.	3
4	The wolfves chased the frightened deer.	4
5	I made three gueses before I got the right answer.	5
6	There are several giraffs in this zoo.	6
7	The leafs are falling from the trees.	7
8	There are four active volcanos in this region.	8
9	The dogs chased the kangaroes across the paddock.	9
10	We took lots of photoes at the picnic.	10
11	The Pacific and Atlantic are large oceanes.	11
12	We saw three foxs last night.	12

Total correct ______
12

Parent/Teacher Signature   Date

Homophones 1

Homophones are a type word of called a homonym. They are words that sound the same but have different spellings and different meanings. Examples: bear (to carry, or a type of animal), bare (barren or naked)

Choose the correct word in the brackets. Write it in the spaces.

1. We painted the ________________ of the house white. (ceiling, sealing)
2. The old house has a well-stocked wine ________________ . (seller, cellar)
3. Are you going to ________________ your golf swing today? (practise, practice)
4. Some believe a ________________ will come to save them. (profit, prophet)
5. They made a considerable ________________ from the sale. (profit, prophet)
6. The winds are sure to ________________ later today. (lesson, lessen)
7. At the party the boy was given lots of ________________ . (presence, presents)
8. Our local ________________ has ordered the road be repaired. (counsel, council)
9. His ________________ at the concert was greatly appreciated. (presence, presents)
10. The sailors are ________________ the boards on the sailing ship with tar. (ceiling, sealing)
11. We must attend football ________________ tonight. (practise, practice)
12. They are not ________________ to come with us. (allowed, aloud)
13. Our teacher gave us an interesting ________________ in good manners. (lesson, lessen)
14. The teachers decided to ________________ the mischievous boy. (counsel, council)
15. After he left school Mike took a job as a ________________ of fine clothes. (seller, cellar)
16. The children sang ________________ in the choir room. (allowed, aloud)

Parent/Teacher Signature Date

Homophones 2

Homophones are a type word of called a homonym. They are words that sound the same but have different spellings and different meanings.
Examples: see (to have sight), sea (body of water)

Look closely at the pairs of homophones in the box.
Write each in its correct sentence.

muscle mussel	**stationary stationery**	**morning mourning**	**father farther**
mist missed	**weather whether**	**patients patience**	**mare mayor**

1. The water birds squabbled over the ________________ they found in the river.
2. We purchased ________________ at the newsagents.
3. I did not know ________________ to go or to stay at home.
4. Canada is ________________ from Australia than New Guinea.
5. When the gun misfired it luckily ________________ the young boy.
6. The newly elected ________________ of our city was born in Vietnam.
7. The family is still ________________ the loss of their pet.
8. You need a lot of ________________ to be a kindergarten teacher.
9. The thick ________________ prevented the plane from taking off.
10. Ethan is exercising the large ________________ in his right arm.
11. The train has remained ________________ for ten minutes.
12. The ________________ at this time of the year is quite changeable.
13. Samantha's ________________ works in a factory near the city.
14. The ________________ took her newborn foal to a quiet place.
15. He was running late for school this ________________.
16. I'm afraid this doctor just has too many ________________ to care for.

Parent/Teacher Signature Date

UNIT 18

Old English root words

In the box are words that have come from Old English. Below are the Old English root words and their meanings. Write the words under the root they would have come from.

wisdom	**beat**	**bandage**	**wag**
battle	**homestead**	**sharp**	**bondage**
scrape	**feed**	**groove**	**instead**
fodder	**wise**	**wagon**	**engrave**
dray	**draught**	**fare**	**ferry**

1. wegan (to move)

____

____

2. sceran (to cut)

____

____

3. beatan (to strike)

____

____

4. faran (to go)

____

____

5. witan (to know)

____

____

6. grafan (to dig)

____

____

7. bindan (to bind)

____

____

8. stede (place)

____

____

9. foda (food)

____

____

10. dragan (to drag)

____

____

Parent/Teacher Signature   Date

UNIT 19

Final unstressed syllables, le and el

Many words end in a similar **el** sound, such as **bottle** and **label**, but the spelling is different.

A Find the words that end in **le** or **el** and write them beside their meaning.

a	n	k	l	e	e	a	g	l	e
c	k	e	n	n	e	l	a	n	b
a	b	o	t	t	l	e	p	o	u
m	s	h	o	v	e	l	p	v	g
e	b	e	e	t	l	e	l	e	l
l	p	a	r	c	e	l	e	l	e

1.fruit ______

2.dog's home ______

3.bird of prey ______

4.large animal ______

5.insect ______

6.foot joint ______

7.musical instrument ______

8.package ______

9.container ______

10.garden tool ______

11.book ______

B Those words that end in **le** or **el** have been cramped up. Find them and write them in the correct sentence below.

junglequarrelbicyclesquirrelturtlegravelkettlebarrelneedletunnel

1. She is riding a ______ around Australia to raise money for a charity.
2. We boiled the water in the ______.
3. The truck and graders spread the ______ over the road.
4. The explorers found it hard to push through the dense ______.
5. A ______ was dug through the mountain for a railway.
6. The wine was matured in a wooden ______.
7. The ______ buried the acorn nuts in readiness for winter.
8. An angry ______ broke out between the two boys.
9. She pricked her finger with the sharp ______.
10. The ______ was kept with the tortoises in the aquarium.

Parent/Teacher Signature Date

UNIT 20

Final unstressed syllables, il and al

Many words end in a similar **el** sound, such as **evil** or **dental**, but the spelling is different.

A Add **al** or **il** in the space at the end of each word to give its correct spelling.

1. ped________ (part of a bike)	4. nostr________ (opening in your nose)	7. penc________ (writing implement)	10. foss________ (old bones)
2. pet________ (part of a flower)	5. per________ (danger)	8. sand________ (footwear)	11. fin________ (last)
3. lent________ (vegetable)	6. gerb________ (rodent)	9. cryst________ (rock particle)	12. mamm________ (type of animal)

B The words in the box contain **al** or **il**. Write each in the correct sentence below.

cordial	**evil**	**council**	**medal**	**tidal**
tonsils	**feral**	**metal**	**central**	**peril**

1. She enjoyed a glass of icy-cold ______________ after sport.
2. Our local city ______________ meets once a month.
3. This river is a ______________ one controlled by the ocean.
4. The small child had her ______________ removed.
5. The government is trying to control ______________ animals in the national park.
6. This new machine is made of a special ______________.
7. The motel was situated in a ______________ part of the city.
8. The ship nearing the rocks was in great ______________.
9. The young soldier was awarded a ______________ for her service.
10. The wicked witch cast an ______________ spell in the fairy tale.

Parent/Teacher Signature Date

Sound patterns, or and oa

A The sound pattern **or** can have four spellings: (a) **or** as in **sword** and **more** (b) **oar** as in **board** (c) **oor** as in **poor** (d) **our** as in **your**. Use a word from the box to fill each space in the sentence.

broad	**enormous**	**sponsor**	**moor**	**core**
floor	**four**	**door**	**roar**	**meteor**

1. She grimaced as she bit into the apple ________________ .
2. She hid behind the ________________ when she heard the intruder.
3. I asked my parents to ________________ me in the fun run.
4. The lion's ________________ made everyone jump.
5. The astronomer followed the path of the ________________ across the sky.
6. He was well known for his ________________ shoulders.
7. There were ________________ students in the group.
8. He had to mop the ________________ after he left his muddy footprints.
9. An elephant is ________________ when compared with a tiny mouse.
10. She was terrified as she walked across the gloomy ________________ .

B Some words with the letter pattern **oa** are pronounced with the long **o** sound, as in **toad**. Choose the correct **oa** word in the brackets to complete each sentence.

1. The baker has seven ________________ of bread in the oven. (loaves, oats)
2. Be careful as you ________________ the old bridge. (poach, approach)
3. Around this castle is a deep ________________. (float, moat)
4. In 1850 a ________________ service ran between the towns. (coach, boast)
5. Mike has a very sore ________________. (bloat, throat)
6. We tried to ________________ the kitten down from the roof. (loam, coax)
7. I had a hot drink of ________________ for my supper. (whoa, cocoa)
8. It was only an April Fool's Day ________________. (hoax, broach)

Parent/Teacher Signature Date

Sound patterns, ea

The letters **ea** can make three sounds:
(a) long **e**, as in **reason** (b) short **e**, as in **thread**
(c) long **a**, as in **great**.

A Use an **ea** (long **e** sound) word from the box to fill the spaces.

dreary	peace	breathe	bleach	conceal
increased	grease	disease	eagle	decrease

1. The two warring countries decided to broker a ______________ treaty.
2. The thief tried to ______________ the whereabouts of the missing jewels.
3. He will often ______________ his hair so it is blond.
4. The thick smoke made it difficult for us to ______________.
5. Jack has ______________ his school grades, which has pleased his teachers.
6. The sea ______________ swooped down and gathered up the fish.
7. We hope road accidents will ______________ now the traffic lights are there.
8. It was just one of these boring, ______________ days.
9. Cancer is no longer an incurable ______________.
10. The mechanic smeared ______________ around the joints of the vehicle.

B Sort the words in the boxes into their three sounds, long **e** **(reason)**, short **e** **(thread)** and long **a** **(great)**.

grease	spread	increase
head	steak	weather
break	least	great

Long e sound	Short e sound	Long a sound
______________	______________	______________
______________	______________	______________
______________	______________	______________

Parent/Teacher Signature Date

UNIT 23

Sound patterns, ir and ur

Some words with an **er** sound pattern are spelled using **ir**, as in **fir**, or **ur**, as in **fur**.

A When the letters **ir** occur in an accented first syllable, as in **circuit** and **girl**, they are pronounced with an **er** sound. Match each word in the box to one it can be linked with in some way.

circle	smirk	stirring	birth	dirty
circus	chirp	thirty	thirsty	circuit

1. clown ____________________
2. bird ____________________
3. square ____________________
4. frown ____________________
5. twenty-nine ____________________
6. baby ____________________
7. clean ____________________
8. car racing ____________________
9. hungry ____________________
10. agitating ____________________

B Many words spelled with **ur** are pronounced with the **er** sound pattern, as in **cur** and **fur**. The **ur** words below have been cramped up. Write each beside the word below that can be linked to it in some way.

surgeonturkeyturtlepurplehurdlesurfersuburbturnip

1. shell ____________________
2. yellow ____________________
3. athlete ____________________
4. operation ____________________
5. city ____________________
6. carrot ____________________
7. Christmas ____________________
8. waves ____________________

Parent/Teacher Signature   Date

UNIT 24

Sound patterns, au and ou

A The letters **au** can represent two sounds:
(a) **or**, as in **sauce** (b) short **o**, as in **sausage**.
Write each word from the box in the correct space in each sentence.

autumn	**auction**	**exhaust**	**gauze**	**cauliflower**
sausage	**authentic**	**nausea**	**automatic**	**tarpaulin**

1. She suffered ________________ from the smell of the chemical.
2. They placed some ________________ around the deep wound.
3. The house was sold at an ________________ last week.
4. In the USA they refer to our ________________ as the fall.
5. The strong ________________ was used to cover the perishable goods.
6. I ate a spicy ________________ at the barbeque.
7. This car does not have a gear stick because it is an ________________ .
8. The ________________ was chopped up ready to cook.
9. The one on the wall is a fake but this one here is quite ________________ .
10. The fumes coming from the ________________ fans permeated the room.

B The letters **ou** have three sounds:
(a) **ow**, as in **devour** (b) long **o**, as in **group** (c) short **u** as in **country**.
Look closely at the words in the box. Write each beside its meaning below.

cougar	**flounder**	**routine**	**acoustics**	**cousin**
mountain	**moustache**	**toucan**	**amount**	**soup**

1. hair below nose ________________
2. kind of fish ________________
3. wild cat ________________
4. colourful bird ________________
5. to do with sound ________________
6. very high hill ________________
7. daily practice ________________
8. watery food ________________
9. relation ________________
10. quantity ________________

Parent/Teacher Signature Date

Revision

A Look closely at the words in the box and then write them under their correct headings below.

hound	**exhaust**	**cousin**	**cauliflower**	**coast**	**auction**
rough	**flounder**	**loaves**	**authentic**	**soup**	**troupe**

au = or (sauce) ____________ ____________

au = short o (sausage) ____________ ____________

ou = short u (country) ____________ ____________

ou = long oo (group) ____________ ____________

ou = ow (devour) ____________ ____________

oa = long o (boat) ____________ ____________

B Add the correct sound pattern in the space.

1. We are going to the c___cus tonight. (**ur**, **ir**)
2. Tom has been appointed c___ch of the team. (**oa**, **ur**)
3. The house is going to be sold by ___ction. (**or**, **au**)
4. Mr Smith keeps the same r___tine everyday. (**or**, **ou**)
5. We caught a lot of fl___nder when we fished from the pier. (**au**, **ou**)
6. The squirr___ stored the nuts for the winter. (**le**, **el**)
7. The sugar cryst___ sweetened the drink. (**il**, **al**)
8. The ship dropped anch___ in the bay. (**er**, **or**)
9. The s___geon decided to operate immediately. (**ir**, **ur**)
10. Thomas Edison was an ingenious invent___. (**er**, **or**)

Parent/Teacher Signature Date

Test 1

The spelling mistakes in these sentences have been underlined. Write the correct spelling for each underlined word on the line.

1	She drew a sircle in her book.	1
2	During ortumn leaves fall from the trees.	2
3	Mr Smith has a mustashe on his face.	3
4	We planted a colliflower in the garden.	4
5	When she tripped she injured her ankel.	5
6	I ride a bicycel to school each day.	6
7	Mum wears leather sandils sometimes.	7
8	Our town councel meets each Thursday.	8
9	The scientists collected the fossels for the museum.	9
10	The large company is a keen sponser of our team.	10
11	The sergeon decided to operate immediately.	11
12	The seed was spred all over the fields.	12

Total correct ______
12

Parent/Teacher Signature

Date

Test 2

Each sentence has one word that is incorrect. Circle the word and write its correct spelling on the line.

1	The exhorst on the car had a hole in it.	1
2	We ate some tomato soop for our tea.	2
3	Cancer is a dreadful diseese.	3
4	The wether at this time of the year is unpredictable.	4
5	The petil on this flower is pink.	5
6	She really enjoyed her glass of cordiel after school.	6
7	Sally plays a bugel in the army.	7
8	A whale is a mammil like a porpoise.	8
9	Mr Jones has never been elected mayer of our city.	9
10	The explorers signed a treety with the native people.	10
11	The racing car charged around the sercuit.	11
12	I am sure this is the finil time we will see her.	12

Total correct ______ / 12

Parent/Teacher Signature　　　　　　　　Date

UNIT 28

Past tense verbs

The spelling of the past tense of verbs is often a difficult concept to grasp.

Most verbs form their tenses in a regular way by simply adding **ed**. Example: Today I pour the drink. Yesterday I poured the drinks.

For some regular verbs you must double the last letter.

Example: chop, chopped

However, irregular verbs don't form the past tense by simply adding **ed** as regular verbs do. Instead, the structure of the verb changes. Examples: Today I bite into the sandwich. Yesterday I bit into the sandwich. Today the cat creeps. Yesterday the cat crept.

A Change the verb in brackets at the end of each sentence into the past tense.

1. Yesterday the butter ________________ in the hot sun. (melt)
2. This morning I ________________ during the maths lesson. (doze)
3. Last night we ________________ the floor of our kitchen. (scrub)
4. The cricketers ________________ five catches during the game. (drop)
5. The burglar was ________________ by the police after the robbery. (catch)
6. The frost ________________ the water in the pipes. (freeze)
7. Jack ________________ a large house at the corner. (build)
8. Our coach ________________ us how to kick the ball. (teach)
9. The Crusaders ________________ before the cross. (kneel)
10. He ________________ our house early this morning. (leave)

B Complete the chart below by adding the correct form of the verb.

1. Today I bake.	Yesterday I __________	7. Today I forget.	Yesterday I __________
2. Today I jump.	Yesterday I __________	8. Today I hide.	Yesterday I __________
3. Today I climb.	Yesterday I __________	9. Today I give.	Yesterday I __________
4. Today I hop.	Yesterday I __________	10. Today I tear.	Yesterday I __________
5. Today I clap.	Yesterday I __________	11. Today I write.	Yesterday I __________
6. Today I choose.	Yesterday I __________	12. Today I swear.	Yesterday I __________

Parent/Teacher Signature Date

Possessives

An apostrophe is used to show ownership of something.
When adding an apostrophe of possession you must remember:

★ If the noun is singular, add an apostrophe and an s at the end. Examples: the car of the teacher, the teacher's car; the dress of the girl, the girl's dress

★ If the noun is plural and ends in s, add the apostrophe after the s. Examples: the leaves of the trees, the trees' leaves; the manes of the horses, the horses' manes

★ If the plural does not end in s, simply add an apostrophe s. In other words, add apostrophe s after you have made the plural. Examples: the pens of the children, the children's pens; the dogs of the men, the men's dogs

Rewrite the phrases showing where the apostrophe should go.

1. the saddles of the cowboy
 ____
2. the legs of the chair
 ____
3. the handlebar of the bicycle
 ____
4. the pages of the book
 ____
5. the bags of the lady
 ____
6. the bags of the ladies
 ____
7. the toys of the children
 ____
8. the homes of the women
 ____
9. the pages of the diaries
 ____
10. the cap of the police officer
 ____
11. the feathers of the geese
 ____
12. the wings of the butterflies
 ____
13. the antenna of the butterfly
 ____
14. the glasses of the men
 ____

Parent/Teacher Signature Date

UNIT 30

Adding the suffix ly

We often add ly to certain words to make them adverbs:

★ For some words there is no change.
Examples: clever, cleverly; poor, poorly

★ For those that end in y, change the y to i and then add ly.
Examples: merry, merrily; steady, steadily

★ For those that end in e, drop the e and then add ly.
Examples: possible, possibly; humble, humbly

★ For words that end in l there is no change. Simply add ly.
Examples: loyal, loyally; fatal, fatally; mental, mentally

Make the word in brackets at the end of each sentence end in ly. As you do them refer to the notes above.

1. Jennifer accepted the award ________________. (proud)
2. The exhausted runner yawned ________________. (weary)
3. The kangaroo ________________ jumped the fence. (easy)
4. The choir sang ________________. (sweet)
5. She signed the letter 'Yours ________________'. (true)
6. The mother cow nudged her calf ________________. (gentle)
7. The children ran through the rooms ________________. (noisy)
8. He traced over the picture ________________. (careful)
9. The committee meets here ________________. (annual)
10. She waited ________________ for the missing puppy. (hopeful)
11. The greedy boy ate the buns ________________. (hungry)
12. She was ________________ upset when she heard the news. (terrible)
13. The awkward boy lifted the boxes ________________. (clumsy)
14. The dog snarled ________________ at the stranger. (angry)
15. We put the toys away ________________. (quick)
16. The old lady rested in the chair ________________. (comfortable)

Parent/Teacher Signature Date

Adding the suffix ion

When adding ion to words ending in ct or ss there are no spelling changes. Example: act + ion = action
If the word ends in te or se drop the e before adding ion. Example: educate + ion = education.

Make the word in brackets end in ion and write the new word in the space.

1. The ________________ of the candidates was fast. (select)
2. Her ________________ was to be expected. (react)
3. The ________________ of the hall took us most of the day. (decorate)
4. The children made an excellent ________________ of the teacher's artwork. (imitate)
5. We are shocked by the ________________ of so many of our native creatures. (extinct)
6. She never ever revealed her ________________ to us. (profess)
7. We felt his work was a great ________________. (create)
8. Mike had a ________________ with the gorillas. (fascinate)
9. The long ________________ marched down the street. (process)
10. The mother fox displays a lot of ________________ towards her cubs. (affect)
11. She made an accurate ________________ that it would be stormy today. (predict)
12. He had an ________________ to strong cheese. (averse)

Write these words in sentences of your own:

separation ________________________________

congratulations ________________________________

repulsion ________________________________

subtraction ________________________________

Parent/Teacher Signature   Date

UNIT 32

Revision

A Add the apostrophe of possession correctly to each noun. The first one has been done for you.

1. the claws of the cat
   the cat's claws
2. the toys of the child
   ____
3. the nests of the birds
   ____
4. the covers of the books
   ____
5. the glasses of the ladies
   ____
6. the dresses of the women
   ____
7. the leaves of the trees
   ____
8. the neck of the giraffe
   ____

B Make the following words end in **ly**. The first one has been done for you.

1. easy *easily*
2. noisy ______________________
3. lucky ______________________
4. drowsy ______________________
5. gentle ______________________
6. idle ______________________
7. possible ______________________
8. probable ______________________

C In the spaces, write the past tense of the verb underlined.

1. Today I <u>swim</u> in the pool but yesterday I ______________________ in the pool.
2. Today I <u>creep</u> in but yesterday I ______________________ in.
3. Today I <u>drink</u> the water but yesterday I ______________________ the water.
4. Today I <u>feel</u> good but yesterday I ______________________ terrible.
5. Today I <u>buy</u> some lollies but yesterday I ______________________ some lollies.
6. Today I <u>ring</u> the bell but yesterday I ______________________ the bell.
7. Today the sun <u>rises</u> early but last month the sun ______________________ late.
8. Today I don't <u>know</u> the answers but yesterday I ______________________ them all.
9. Today I <u>write</u> a story but yesterday I ______________________ a story.
10. Today I <u>leave</u> at 12 o'clock but yesterday I ______________________ at 2 o'clock.

Parent/Teacher Signature Date

Test

The underlined word in each sentence has a mistake. Write the word correctly in the space.

	Sentence	Answer
1	Yesterday I <u>choped</u> the wood for my uncle.	1
2	Our teacher <u>taut</u> us how to make puppets.	2
3	Last night the water in the pipes <u>freeze</u>.	3
4	The <u>ladie's</u> dresses are in the wardrobe.	4
5	The <u>butterflys'</u> wings were damaged.	5
6	The starving boy ate the food <u>greedyly</u>.	6
7	The savage dog snarled <u>angryly</u> at the stranger.	7
8	She signed the letter 'Yours <u>truely</u>'.	8
9	She lifted the puppy <u>gentily</u>.	9
10	Ben <u>dropt</u> lots of catches when playing cricket.	10
11	The <u>childrens'</u> toys are in the room.	11
12	The <u>childs'</u> book has been stolen.	12

Total correct ______ / 12

Parent/Teacher Signature　　　　　　　　Date

Homographs

Homographs are a type of word called a homonym. Homographs are spelled alike but have different meanings and different pronunciation. Examples: desert (dry barren area), desert (to abandon or leave) tear (to rip up), tear (produced when you cry)

Use the homograph from the box to fill each space. Ensure you know how it is pronounced each time. An **n** denotes it being used as a noun and a **v** denotes it being used as a verb. Note after each sentence whether the word is a noun or a verb.

desert (n)	**record (n)**	**permit (n)**	**rebel (n)**	**subject (n)**	**combat (n)**
desert (v)	**record (v)**	**permit (v)**	**rebel (v)**	**subject (v)**	**combat (v)**

1. I wonder if they will ______________ us to park the car here.
2. The runner created a new 100-metre ______________.
3. The explorers perished in the sand-blown ______________.
4. The pop group is going to ______________ a new song this month.
5. The students felt it was their right to ______________ against the unfair laws.
6. They will ______________ the captured soldier to a great deal of cruel treatment.
7. What is the main ______________ you are studying this year?
8. This medicine will ______________ the side effects of your disease.
9. The soldiers saw a lot of ______________ during the war.
10. You now need a valid ______________ to enter this building.
11. The explorers decided to ______________ their comrades and leave them to the dangers of hunger and thirst.
12. The ______________ was arrested in the jungle camp.

Parent/Teacher Signature Date

Contractions

A contraction is formed when one or more letters are omitted from a word and replaced with an apostrophe. Examples: We are not going. = We aren't going. She is not home. = She isn't home.

Rewrite each sentence in A, replacing the contraction with the two words it is made from. In B, make a contraction from the two underlined words.

A

1. It's always hot in summer.
   ____
2. Jack didn't do it.
   ____
3. We've got to hurry.
   ____
4. I'm sure she will win the game.
   ____
5. Hurry up because we're leaving soon.
   ____
6. I am sure that's the one.
   ____
7. I don't think you're being fair.
   ____
8. What's the time?
   ____

B

1. She is the only one left.
   ____
2. I have just enough time left.
   ____
3. There is a lot of noise here.
   ____
4. I think they will help us.
   ____
5. I do not think it is right.
   ____
6. You would be warmer in a thick coat.
   ____
7. She said they are not coming now.
   ____
8. We would have won except for the umpire.
   ____

Parent/Teacher Signature Date

Latin root words

Some words we use have come from the language of the ancient Romans, which is called Latin.

Look at the words in the box. In the space, write the word formed from the Latin root word and its meaning.

fortress	**dentist**	**proprietor**	**conductor**	**current**	**missile**
culprit	**actor**	**abbreviate**	**operate**	**factory**	**signature**

1. The nuclear ________________ was fired from the ship. (mitto = I send)
2. The strong ________________ swept the swimmers downstream. (curro = I run)
3. The ________________ took us to our seats. (duco = I lead)
4. The surgeon said she would have to ________________ to remove the bullet. (opus = work)
5. My uncle works in a large ________________ that produces cars. (facio = I make)
6. She is the ________________ of this store. (proprius = one's own)
7. The film star wrote her ________________ on the book. (signum = mark)
8. They will ________________ the story. (brevis = short)
9. I visited the ________________ to see about my aching tooth. (dens = tooth)
10. When she leaves school she hopes to become an ________________. (actum = I act)
11. The knights built a huge ________________. (fortis = strong)
12. The ________________ was soon caught by the police. (culpa = fault)

Parent/Teacher Signature Date

Final unstressed syllables, et and it

Many words end in a similar **et** sound, such as **cricket** and **credit**, but the spelling is different.

Add the syllable **et** or **it** to the incomplete word in each sentence.

1. We filled the buck____ with water.
2. Our school fete made quite a good prof____ on the day.
3. When we reached the summ____ we sat and rested.
4. Oliver is learning to play the trump____.
5. Emily's wall____ was stolen by a brazen thief.
6. We came across the herm____ in the deep jungle.
7. It was so cold I asked for another blank____ for my bed.
8. This robin has beautiful scarl____ feathers on its chest.
9. The accountants were conducting an aud____ of the money.
10. There was a lot of mer____ in Joel's performance.
11. The satellite was sent into orb____ around the Earth.
12. The school works to a strict budg____.
13. This mixture of metal and cloth is a very strange gadg____.
14. In the work areas you must always wear a helm____.
15. The doctor advised the patient to take one tabl____ a day.
16. The poisonous berries caused him to vom____.

Write these words in sentences of your own:

jacket ______________________________

rabbit ______________________________

bandit ______________________________

fidget ______________________________

Parent/Teacher Signature Date

UNIT 38

Final unstressed syllables, ar and or

Some words with an **er** sound pattern are spelled using **ar**, as in **scholar**, or **or**, as in **actor**.

Add **ar** or **or** to complete the words in each sentence.

1. The aeroplane is waiting in the hang____.
2. We could see the mete____ through our telescope.
3. She cut the paper with the sciss____s.
4. My younger brother has a tut____ for mathematics.
5. The electricity here comes from sol____ power.
6. The nurse shaved his chest with a raz____.
7. The dentist said a mol____ had to be extracted.
8. We hid the valuables in the cell____.
9. The edit____ of the paper dismissed the report.
10. The wealthy person gave the begg____ some money.
11. The may____ of our city is from Vietnam.
12. The coug____ crept stealthily after the baby deer.
13. I welcomed the visit____ to our school.
14. A large ced____ tree grew in the back yard.
15. The butterflies searched for the nect____ of the flowers.
16. The curs____ on the computer operated the search.

Write these words in sentences of your own:

lunar ____________________

scholar ____________________

terror ____________________

tremor ____________________

Parent/Teacher Signature Date

Silent letters

Silent (or unsounded) letters occur in some words. This is often because they were once sounded in the word.

A All the words in the grid contain a silent letter. Find the words and complete each sentence.

s	g	n	a	t	b
c	c	h	c	y	e
e	o	o	a	o	r
n	m	u	l	l	e
t	b	r	f	k	t

1. I tidied my hair with a ________________.
2. There are sixty minutes in one ________________.
3. The yellow part of an egg is called the ________________.
4. A soft flat cap is a ________________.
5. This flower has a very strong ________________.
6. I slapped the ________________ away with my hand.

B Write the word in each group that contains a silent letter. Circle the silent letter.

1. cover, tape, scissors ________________
2. scheme, plan, atlas ________________
3. table, joke, wren ________________
4. balloon, depot, folder ________________
5. paper, sword, book ________________
6. ruin, wreck, bold ________________
7. dinghy, boat, clock ________________
8. jockey, plan, tomb ________________
9. glasses, book, wrist ________________
10. pencil, guard, hair ________________

C Write each word beside its definition. Circle the silent letter in each word.

honest	**hymn**	**knives**	**thumb**	**science**
handsome	**wreath**	**answer**	**aisle**	**sword**

1. school subject ________________
2. digit of the hand ________________
3. cutting implements ________________
4. song of praise ________________
5. trustworthy ________________
6. space between seats ________________
7. steel weapon ________________
8. opposite to question ________________
9. ring of flowers ________________
10. good looking ________________

Parent/Teacher Signature Date

UNIT 40

Consonant groups, ph and gh as an f sound

The consonant group ph is always pronounced as an f sound (**photo** and **graph**). The gh group is sometimes pronounced as an f (**rough**), but not always (**bough** and **ghost**, for example, are exceptions).

Complete the sentences below with a word from the box.

cough	**photograph**	**dolphin**	**nephew**	**tough**	**rough**
laughter	**pharmacy**	**graph**	**sphere**	**enough**	**aphids**

1. The insecticide soon destroyed the _______________ on the roses.
2. This paper is smooth but that one is _______________.
3. James is my favourite _______________.
4. Sally drew a _______________ in her exercise book in maths.
5. She is taking medicine for her _______________.
6. There was a lot of happy _______________ coming from the classroom.
7. The _______________ was kept in the large aquarium.
8. When she counted the cars she made a _______________ of the results.
9. Don't give me any more because I have _______________.
10. The steak I was given was quite _______________ to chew.
11. I took a _______________ of my whole family.
12. We bought the tablets at the _______________.

Write these words in sentences of your own:

elephant ____

laugh ____

trophy ____

alphabet ____

Parent/Teacher Signature Date

Complex consonant groups, ch and tch, dge and ge

The letter groups **ch** and **tch** are pronounced the same (**such** and **fetch**), as are **dge** and **ge** (**dodge** and **cage**). Note: All of the consonant groups come after a short vowel, except **ge**, which isn't strictly a consonant group but acts as one.

Add **ch**, **tch**, **dge** or **ge** in the spaces to complete each word.

1. Be careful or the kitten might scra______ you.
2. Around the house is a neatly cut he______.
3. The bar______ carried the wool along the river.
4. He proudly wears the ba______ given to him by his uncle.
5. The chocolate mud cake was extremely ri______.
6. The scientist made a rough ske______ of the equipment.
7. We measured three millimetres of rain in the gau______.
8. The spilt ink left a large smu______ in her book.
9. The stubborn donkey would not bu______.
10. We made a delicious sandwi______ for lunch.
11. The ju______ sentenced the burglar to two years in prison.
12. We heard a stran______ noise coming from the room.
13. A stream of water ran along the di______.
14. The hen sat on its clu______ of eggs.
15. In football you must do______ your opponent.
16. You should not bear a gru______ against those who hurt you.

Parent/Teacher Signature

Date

UNIT 42

Syllables

A syllable is a unit of sound. It contains one sounded vowel only. The vowel may be preceded by or followed by several consonants.

A In each set, put the syllables in order to make the word described.

1. con ded clu (finished) ________________
2. ger dan ous (perilous) ________________
3. es nec sary (vital, needed) ________________
4. ton as ish (surprise) ________________
5. dile o croc (reptile) ________________
6. gle rec tan (shape) ________________
7. en cal dar (yearly dates) ________________
8. to oc pus (sea creature) ________________
9. ous num er (many) ________________
10. ue con tin (to go on) ________________
11. ture ad ven (exciting time) ________________
12. lem ade on (soft drink) ________________
13. se mu um (display centre) ________________
14. tion ca va (holiday) ________________
15. wear der un (clothing) ________________
16. to po ta (edible tuber) ________________

B Write the following words, separating their syllables:

1. ordinary ________________
2. following ________________
3. chocolate ________________
4. possessive ________________

Parent/Teacher Signature Date

Revision

A Add the correct ending to complete each word.

1. bask ________ (container)
2. prof ________ (to gain)
3. chedd ________ (kind of cheese)
4. sug ________ (sweetener)
5. raz ________ (cutting blade)
6. hatch ________ (small axe)
7. ex ________ (way out)
8. fauc ________ (tap)
9. trait ________ (person who betrays their country)
10. lun ________(to do with the moon)

B Add the missing silent letter in each word.

1. ren (small bird) ________________
2. tom (grave) ________________
3. hansome (good looking) ________________
4. iland (land surrounded by water) ________________
5. nife (cutting blade) ________________
6. sceme (a plan) ________________
7. nat (small insect) ________________
8. yok (yellow of an egg) ________________
9. sent (perfume) ________________
10. autum (season) ________________

C Write the following words, separating their three syllables.

1. telephone ________________
2. rapidly ________________
3. elephant ________________
4. securely ________________
5. interview ________________
6. furniture ________________
7. kerosene ________________
8. indignant ________________
9. circulate ________________
10. contested ________________

Parent/Teacher Signature   Date

Test 1

Each sentence has one word that is incorrect. Circle the word and then write its correct spelling on the line.

1	The satellite was sent into orbet around the Earth.	1
2	This is a strange-looking little gadjit.	2
3	The wallit was stolen by the pickpocket.	3
4	The bandet was soon caught by the posse.	4
5	Riley welcomed the visiter to our school.	5
6	We run our fans on electricity from solor power.	6
7	She is now the editar of the newspaper.	7
8	Jack is my favourite nefew.	8
9	There is a large farmacy in this street.	9
10	She made a quick skech of the bridge.	10
11	We cut the paper with the sissors.	11
12	The gard told the people to stop.	12

Total correct ______ / 12

Parent/Teacher Signature   Date

Test 2

The spelling mistakes in these sentences have been underlined. Write the correct spelling for each word in the box.

	Sentence	Answer
1	The jugde sentenced the criminal to jail.	1
2	He rowed across the river in a dingy.	2
3	This shop makes a good profet each week.	3
4	A couger is a large sleek cat.	4
5	We packed the food in the baskit.	5
6	Do not strech your muscles too much.	6
7	The hen has laid a cluch of eggs.	7
8	He takes a vitamin tablit each day.	8
9	When he tripped he broke his rist.	9
10	She wrote the anser in her book.	10
11	The dolfin was kept in the aquarium.	11
12	There was a lot of lafter coming from the room.	12

Total correct ______
12

Parent/Teacher Signature Date

UNIT 46

Doubling, adding ed

When a word ends in two consonants and you want to add the suffix ed, no letters are doubled.
Example: mend, mended

If the word ends in a consonant with one vowel before it, double the last consonant before adding ed.
Example: hop, hopped

When a word ends with a silent e, drop the e before adding ed. Example: wave, waved

Add ed to the words in the brackets and write them in the blanks.

1. The kangaroo ________________ across the paddock. (hop)
2. We ________________ off the lights when we left. (switch)
3. The dog ________________ the car. (chase)
4. We ________________ the side of the house. (paint)
5. The accident ________________ at the corner. (occur)
6. I have ________________ my money to buy a new bicycle. (save)
7. I ________________ the newly ripened apricots. (taste)
8. The falling boy ________________ the branch of the tree. (grip)
9. Sophie ________________ in all subjects. (excel)
10. The doctor ________________ him to a specialist. (refer)
11. The rocket ________________ the moon. (orbit)
12. I ________________ my choice to just three. (adjust)
13. The student ________________ her assignment to the teacher. (submit)
14. The workers ________________ the hinges on the door. (change)
15. The hungry dog ________________ for the biscuit. (beg)
16. The concert ________________ for two hours. (last)

Parent/Teacher Signature   Date

Doubling, adding ing

When a word ends in two consonants and you want to add the suffix ing, no letters are doubled.
Example: last, lasting

If the word ends in a consonant with one vowel before it, double the last consonant before adding ing.
Example: hop, hopping

When a words ends with a silent e, drop the e when adding ing. Example: drive, driving

Make the word in brackets end in ing.

1. The workers are _______________ down the trees. (chop)
2. The students are _______________ off the lamps before leaving the room. (switch)
3. The adults are _______________ on the chairs near the door. (sit)
4. The professor is _______________ to the students. (lecture)
5. The activities are all _______________ in the gymnasium. (occur)
6. The spectators are _______________ loudly. (clap)
7. The people are _______________ in the ballroom. (dance)
8. Josh is _______________ lots of butterflies. (catch)
9. Max is _______________ in all subjects this year. (excel)
10. He wasn't talking about horses; he was _______________ to donkeys. (refer)
11. The satellite is _______________ the Earth. (orbit)
12. We are _______________ the field to only ten competitors. (limit)
13. The students are now _______________ their demands to the directors. (submit)
14. The police are _______________ the culprit to surrender. (advise)
15. The bombs are _______________ in the city. (explode)
16. They keep _______________ me for all the noise. (blame)

Parent/Teacher Signature Date

Adding ion to base words

When you add the suffix ion to words that end in te, drop the e before adding ion. If the word ends in de, change the de to s before adding ion. Examples: devote + ion = devotion; divide + ion = division

Make the word in brackets fit the meaning of the sentence, making sure that your spelling is correct.

1. There was a loud ________________ in the laboratory. (explode)
2. This is only an ________________ of the real thing. (imitate)
3. He gave a large ________________ to our school. (donate)
4. A great deal of ________________ has occurred here. (pollute)
5. The ________________ of the hall for the dance is done. (decorate)
6. This is a good ________________ to film the movie. (locate)
7. The surgeon performed the ________________ in the theatre. (operate)
8. This newspaper has a large ________________ in the city. (circulate)
9. The sculpture was an excellent ________________. (create)
10. She wrote the ________________ of the words in a book. (translate)
11. She said her ________________ was final. (decide)
12. I hope to attend Michelle's ________________ from university. (graduate)
13. The ________________ woke the whole neighbourhood. (collide)
14. The ________________ work in this book is beautiful. (illustrate)
15. The ________________ of the gully was quite severe. (erode)
16. The ________________ caused by the wind rattled the crockery. (vibrate)

Parent/Teacher Signature Date

Adjectives and nouns, ance or ant endings

Adjectives can be formed by making a word end in **ant**. Abstract nouns can be formed by making the word end in **ance**. Choose the correct word, either the noun or the adjective, to write in the space.

1. Even though the storm has passed we must remain ________________. (vigilant, vigilance)
2. There was a great deal of ________________ to help the teacher. (reluctant, reluctance)
3. The ________________ of the roses was appreciated by all. (fragrant, fragrance)
4. It took only an ________________ for the bomb to explode. (instant, instance)
5. We must always be prepared to be ________________ of all religions. (tolerant, tolerance)
6. The boy's reaction was one of hostile ________________ . (defiant, defiance)
7. The mole on his shoulder was thought to be ________________ (malignant, malignance)
8. I could not see the ________________ of his stupid suggestion. (relevant, relevance)
9. She is really a spoilt ________________ child. (petulant, petulance)
10. The ________________ of the bright light temporarily blinded us. (brilliant, brilliance)
11. The lady looked quite ________________ in her silk dress. (elegant, elegance)
12. The young boy's ________________ during the game impressed the coach. (exuberant, exuberance)
13. This material is completely ________________ to any moisture. (resistant, resistance)
14. The lady's ________________ amazed all of us. (extravagant, extravagance)
15. The ________________ of the scientists' discovery was not readily appreciated. (significant, significance)
16. The boy who noticed the change must be very ________________. (observant, observance)

Parent/Teacher Signature Date

UNIT 50

Revision

A Look closely at the words in the box. Add **ed** to each and write them in two groups, those that simply add **ed** and those that double the last letter when **ed** is added.

drop	travel	chop	weed
skip	play	help	clap
paint	crawl	last	hop

+ ed (no change) ______ ______ ______ ______ ______ ______

+ ed (double last letter) ______ ______ ______ ______ ______ ______

B Look closely at the words in the box. Adding **ing** to each word, sort them into the three groups below.

crawl	travel	push	drive
hope	wash	occur	sleep
spot	write	use	swim

+ ing (drop final e) ______ ______ ______ ______

+ ing (no change) ______ ______ ______ ______

+ ing (double last letter) ______ ______ ______ ______

C Complete these words with the word endings **ant** or **ion**. Sort them into the two groups below.

vigil______	locat______	malign______	translat______
decorat______	petul______	migrat______	eleg______

+ ant ______ ______ ______ ______

+ ion ______ ______ ______ ______

Parent/Teacher Signature Date

Test

Choose the correct spelling from the words in brackets.

1	The wallabies (hopt, hopped) over the hedge.	1
2	The dogs are (chaseing, chasing) the cats.	2
3	The accident (occurred, occured) at the corner.	3
4	The police are (advising, adviseing) us to leave.	4
5	The bombs are (exploding, explodeing).	5
6	There is a great deal of (pollushen, pollution).	6
7	This newspaper has a large (circulation, circulashun).	7
8	The insects are (resisten, resistant) to chemicals.	8
9	You must be (vigilent, vigilant) in this part of the city.	9
10	The rich people led an (extravagant, extravagent) life.	10
11	She is a very (petulent, petulant) child.	11
12	There was a lot of (resistance, resistence) to his idea.	12

Total correct ______
12

Parent/Teacher Signature Date

UNIT 52

Compound words

By joining two or more words together, we can make a single compound word that replaces a much longer phrase. At first, the compound word may be hyphenated but, when it becomes accepted, the hyphen is dropped to form a single word. Example: web site, web-site, website.

A Find words in the grid that can be added to the words below and write the new compound words on the lines.

w	a	c	h	e	t
h	c	c	c	p	r
e	a	a	o	o	u
r	s	k	a	s	c
e	e	e	t	t	k
b	u	r	g	e	r
f	l	y	s	e	t

1. butter ______________
2. suit ______________
3. pan ______________
4. over ______________
5. sign ______________
6. sun ______________
7. every ______________
8. tooth ______________
9. ham ______________
10. tow ______________

B Lots of compound words contain the names of body parts. Add a body part in the space to make a compound word. Example: tooth + ache = toothache

1. ________ + ball = ________
2. ________ + brush = ________
3. ________ + cuffs = ________
4. ________ + chair = ________
5. ________ + bone = ________
6. ________ + diver = ________
7. ________ + brow = ________
8. ________ + nail = ________

C Join words from Box B to the end of those in Box A to make compound words and write them on the lines below.

Box A	**earth**	**note**	**sun**	**moon**
	sea	**skate**	**sign**	**hay**

Box B **book** **fever** **post** **horse** **burn** **quake** **light** **board**

1. ____________
2. ____________
3. ____________
4. ____________
5. ____________
6. ____________
7. ____________
8. ____________

Parent/Teacher Signature Date

Vowel alternations

When we add suffixes to some words, the vowel sound changes from long to short.
Example: cave (long a), cavity (short a)

Change the word in the brackets so it fits the meaning of the sentence.

1. A long ________________ of people marched down the street. (proceed)
2. Lachlan has a great deal of ________________ in athletics. (able)
3. This food is made from ________________ products. (nature)
4. The young achiever received his ________________ from his elder brother. (inspire)
5. The worker handed in her ________________ to the company manager. (resign)
6. Sally is now the ________________ of a large multinational company. (preside)
7. I have a great deal of ________________ for her achievements. (admire)
8. The ________________ of the heat along the iron rod was quite quick. (conduce)
9. The company has made a big ________________ in its workforce. (reduce)
10. The increased ________________ has been due to the hard work of the staff. (produce)
11. She wrote a long ________________ about dinosaurs. (compose)
12. The explorers suffered great ________________ because of their lack of supplies. (deprive)
13. The teachers made a ________________ that the classrooms would be out of bounds. (decide)
14. A new ________________ moved in next door. (reside)
15. Mia is a close ________________ of our family. (relate)
16. The adults made an equal ________________ of food among all the children. (divide)

Parent/Teacher Signature Date

UNIT 54

Greek root words

Many of the words we use in English come from the base or root of the ancient Greek language. For example from the Greek **polis**, which meant city, we get words like civic, metropolis, policy, politics.

A Write the word from the box that has come from each Greek word below.

electric	**democracy**	**monopoly**	**metre**	**autograph**
calligraphy	**dynamite**	**biologist**	**geology**	**asterisk**

1. **autos** = self ____________
2. **grapho** = I write ____________
3. **aster** = star ____________
4. **bios** = life ____________
5. **monos** = alone ____________
6. **demos** = people ____________
7. **metron** = measure ____________
8. **dunamis** = power ____________
9. **elektron** = amber ____________
10. **geo** = earth ____________

B Write the words we use that have come from these Greek root words.

1. **tele** = far away + **skopeo** = I see ____________
2. **bi** = two + **kyklos** = wheel ____________
3. **alpha** = first letter + **beta** = second letter ____________
4. A car that changes gear by itself comes from the Greek word **auto**, meaning self ____________.
5. A popular board game gets its name from the Greek word **monos**, meaning alone ____________.

C Complete each sentence by making a word from the Greek root in brackets.

1. The (**aster** = star) ____________ studied the planets using a telescope.
2. I took a (**photos** = light) ____________ with my camera.
3. We watched the cartoon on (**tele** = far away) ____________ last night.
4. He studied the germs under the (**micros** = small) ____________.

Parent/Teacher Signature Date

Hard and soft g

The words in the box begin with a hard g, as in **get**, or a soft g, as in **gem**.

Complete the sentences below by choosing the correct word from the box. Tick (✓) those that begin with a hard g and put a cross (✗) beside those that begin with a soft g. There are eight of each.

guitar genie gutter gyrate genius goggles giraffe guilty
gadget gypsy gorilla gesture gossip giant gully general

1. The tiny thing made of metal is a fascinating ________________.
2. Famous physicist Albert Einstein was truly a ________________.
3. In the fairytale a ________________ appears when the lamp is rubbed.
4. Because of the dust he decided to wear ________________.
5. The water from the roof was directed away in the deep ________________.
6. The miners searched for gold in the ________________ between the hills.
7. In this dance the partners must ________________ their hips.
8. After joining the army he one day became a ________________.
9. In a kind ________________ she gave the charity a big donation.
10. We will not tolerate idle ________________ in our group.
11. To relax he sat and strummed his ________________.
12. The ________________ moved his caravan to a new place.
13. The huge ________________ is the largest of the ape family.
14. The judge found the burglar ________________.
15. The newborn ________________ was unsteady on its awkward legs.
16. The legend tells of a mythical ________________.

Parent/Teacher Signature Date

UNIT 56

Hard and soft c

The following words begin with either a hard c, as in **cut**, or a soft c, as in **city**.

Complete each sentence below by choosing the correct word from the box. Tick (✓) those that begin with a hard c and put a cross (✗) beside those that begin with a soft c sound. There are eight of each.

campus	**certain**	**cactus**	**coffee**
circus	**cereal**	**circular**	**census**
cement	**cockatoo**	**citizen**	**cider**
counterfeit	**culprit**	**candidate**	**camouflage**

1. She had a drink of apple ________________.
2. A ________________ has adapted to the dry desert conditions.
3. I enjoy eating my ________________ for breakfast.
4. The police soon apprehended the ________________.
5. The ________________ money was found near a printing press.
6. The footpath had been made of gravel and ________________.
7. My uncle is standing as a ________________ in the election.
8. The outside of the gadget is ________________ in shape.
9. A ________________ of the population was conducted.
10. The students gathered in the ________________ of the university.
11. The soldiers wore uniforms that would ________________ them.
12. The refugee is now a registered ________________ of the country.
13. You must be ________________ of your facts before accusing her.
14. Tom's pet ________________ has lost a lot of feathers.
15. We enjoyed the antics of the clowns at the ________________.
16. It is unwise to drink too many cups of ________________ each day.

Parent/Teacher Signature   Date

Sound patterns, oi, oy and ei

A The two-letter phonograms oi and oy are always pronounced as oy, as in **boy** (oi is never used at the end of a word in English). Use an oi word on the left to complete each sentence.

disappoint
poisonous
joint
avoid
voice
appoint
moist
loiter

1. These clothes are dry but these are still ________________.
2. The young girl has a wonderful singing ________________.
3. You should ________________ any contact with the dangerous chemical.
4. Sophie's rude attitude can really ________________ us at times.
5. The ________________ of your arm is called the elbow.
6. The police will not allow people to ________________ around here.
7. The snake is an extremely ________________ species.
8. The teacher decided to ________________ Alice as our class teacher.

B The two-letter phonogram ei can sound as a long e, as in **deceit**, or a long a, as in **eight**. Use the correct word from the box to complete each sentence below.

ceiling	**receipt**	**neither**	**deceive**	**weight**
neigh	**sleigh**	**seize**	**conceited**	**vein**

1. I asked for a tax ________________ for the goods I purchased.
2. We call the sound of a horse a ________________.
3. I am sure ________________ John nor Sally will help us.
4. The miners discovered a rich ________________ of gold in the rocks.
5. The ________________ of this metal chair makes it difficult to carry.
6. We rode down the snow slope in a ________________.
7. The eagle tried to ________________ the rabbit in its talons.
8. The thief tried to ________________ the rich person.
9. I found the new student to be difficult and ________________.
10. The ________________ of this room needs painting.

Parent/Teacher Signature   Date

UNIT 58

Sound patterns, g as a j sound

The letter **g** is often pronounced as a **j** sound, as in **cage**.

Choose a word from the box to match each meaning below.

carriage	**voyage**	**storage**	**courage**
pigeon	**engine**	**legend**	**gorgeous**
angel	**budget**	**savage**	**sausage**
village	**dungeon**	**margin**	**fragile**

1. a small town ______________________
2. a long trip on a ship ______________________
3. a bird ______________________
4. an underground cell for prisoners ______________________
5. mince meat in a casing ______________________
6. easily broken ______________________
7. bravery, heroism ______________________
8. an ancient story ______________________
9. a heavenly being ______________________
10. angry, vicious ______________________
11. side of a page ______________________
12. very attractive ______________________
13. motor ______________________
14. a vehicle in which to travel ______________________
15. space to keep things ______________________
16. a money plan ______________________

Write these words in your own sentences:

magic ____

message ____

Parent/Teacher Signature Date

Sond patterns, er

The **er** sound can be represented by many different spellings, such as in the second syllable of **fever**, **flavour** and **actor**, or the first syllable of **survive**, **thirteen** or **certain**.

Use the correct word from the box to complete each sentence below.

certain	**vermin**	**interrupt**	**cutlery**
reverse	**interfere**	**encountered**	**desert**
turkey	**liberty**	**rhinoceros**	**thirsty**
preserve	**survive**	**surround**	**surprise**

1. People sometimes use salt to ________________ meat.
2. The boy opened the cage door to give the bird its ________________.
3. The lions began to ________________ the injured deer.
4. The desert explorers began to feel hungry and ________________.
5. Be ________________ of the facts before making that claim.
6. For Christmas lunch we ate a ________________.
7. The massive ________________ charged at the hunters.
8. We ________________ a few issues settling in to the new school.
9. The car began to ________________ out of the garage.
10. It is rude to ________________ when another is speaking.
11. The arid, dry ________________ has claimed many lives.
12. We placed the ________________ around the table ready for lunch.
13. ________________ such as rabbits and rats damage crops.
14. It is unwise to ________________ in other people's affairs.
15. It is hard to ________________ in those dreadful conditions.
16. I got a ________________ seeing Joe as I had not seen him for five years.

Write these words in your own sentences:

mystery ____

verse ____

Parent/Teacher Signature Date

UNIT 60

Sound patterns, y as a long i sound

The letter y is often pronounced as a long i sound, as in **cry** and **reply**.

Match each word in the box to its meaning below.

python	**hyphen**	**hygiene**	**hydrant**
cyclone	**tyrant**	**nylon**	**rhyming**
amplify	**reply**	**defy**	**magnify**
stylish	**cycle**	**bypass**	**beautify**

1. a large snake ______________________
2. answer to a question ______________________
3. words that sound the same ______________________
4. to make louder ______________________
5. to make bigger ______________________
6. a strong destructive wind ______________________
7. a punctuation mark ______________________
8. an artificial fibre ______________________
9. water outlet ______________________
10. to improve the look of something ______________________
11. to go around ______________________
12. a cruel leader ______________________
13. cleanliness, good health ______________________
14. to ride a bike ______________________
15. to disobey an order ______________________
16. modern, good-looking ______________________

Write these words in your own sentences:

supply ____

rely ____

Parent/Teacher Signature   Date

Revision

A Sort the words in the box under the headings below.

gypsy	goggles	guilty	gossip
guitar	giraffe	genius	giant

Hard g sound ____________ ____________

____________ ____________

Soft g sound ____________ ____________

____________ ____________

B Sort the words in the box under the headings below.

cider	cement	coffee	cereal
cockatoo	cactus	citizen	camouflage

Hard c sound ____________ ____________

____________ ____________

Soft c sound ____________ ____________

____________ ____________

C Sort the words in the box under the headings below.

weight	seize	eighty	ceiling
receipt	sleigh	deceive	neigh

Long a sound ____________ ____________

____________ ____________

Long e sound ____________ ____________

____________ ____________

Parent/Teacher Signature Date

Test 1

One word in each sentence is spelled incorrectly. Find that word and write it correctly on the line.

1	We believed the clever man to be a true jenious.	1
2	You must always be sertain of your facts.	2
3	The kockatoo was kept in a large aviary.	3
4	The government took a sensus of the population.	4
5	The eagle tried to seeze the young rabbit.	5
6	The needle punctured a vane of his body.	6
7	We ate a pork sosaje for lunch.	7
8	He told us about many interesting Aboriginal lejends.	8
9	It is unwise to intafere in the affairs of others.	9
10	I am feeling very thursty and need a drink now.	10
11	The large, powerful pithon crushed its prey.	11
12	The officer checked the fire hidrant in the street.	12

Total correct ______
12

Parent/Teacher Signature Date

Test 2

Circle the correct spelling of the word in each group.

1 bicycle, bycicle, bycycle

2 styleish, stilish, stylish

3 turky, turkey, turkee

4 cutlery, cutelry, cuterly

5 serprise, surprise, cerprise

6 voyage, voyige, voiage

7 apointt, apoint, appoint

8 disappoint, dissapoint, dissappoint

9 voice, voise, vocie

10 sereal, cerial, cereal

11 gineus, genius, jeneas

12 guitar, juitar, guitare

13 servive, survive, cervive

14 generil, general, jeneral

15 sitizen, citizan, citizen

16 receipt, reciept, receept

Total correct ______ / 16

Parent/Teacher Signature   Date

UNIT 64

Adding the suffix ary

Adding the suffix ary changes the form of a word or a root word. Sometimes ary changes a noun to an adjective (**custom**, **customary**) or to a different noun form (**sal**, the Latin root word for salt, **salary**). Adding ary can also change a verb to an adjective (**imagine**, **imaginary**) or a verb to a noun (**burgle**, **burglary**).

Add a word from the box to complete each sentence.

necessary	**vocabulary**	**imaginary**	**documentary**
salary	**burglary**	**anniversary**	**diary**
temporary	**stationary**	**solitary**	**boundary**
elementary	**secretary**	**revolutionary**	**customary**

1. It is ____________________ for the bride and groom to kiss.
2. Michelle is the ____________________ to the company manager.
3. It is thought he has at least 10,000 words in his ____________________.
4. Next year Cooper attends ____________________ school.
5. It is ____________________ for us to clean the room before leaving.
6. The train is ____________________ at the station.
7. A ____________________ took place and the jewellery is missing.
8. She now earns a ____________________ of over $100,000.
9. The invention at the time was quite ____________________.
10. The children must stay within the school ____________________.
11. I write what happened every day in a ____________________.
12. Next year is our school's fiftieth ____________________.
13. The television crew is making a nature ____________________.
14. The ____________________ road block will be moved next week.
15. A unicorn does not actually exist; it is just ____________________.
16. A hermit lives a ____________________ life.

Parent/Teacher Signature   Date

Assimilated or absorbed prefixes

Some prefixes become disguised in a word and it is sometimes difficult to tell if it is a prefix or just part of the normal spelling of the word.

The following words all contain prefixes. Use each to complete a sentence below.

immature	**excavate**	**sufficient**	**corrugated**
subscription	**adjective**	**exhaust**	**combined**
difficult	**attention**	**surrender**	**collision**
illegible	**impartial**	**obstinate**	**disregarded**

1. Mike's yearly ____________________ to the magazine cost $40.
2. In grammar, a describing word is called an ____________________.
3. A mule is said to be a stubborn and ____________________ animal.
4. The teacher demanded the boys pay ____________________.
5. Mia completely ____________________ the feelings of others.
6. The problems on the last page were the most ____________________.
7. Her writing is so untidy it is quite ____________________.
8. An umpire or referee should always be fair and ____________________.
9. Jack is the most ____________________ boy I know.
10. The miners will ____________________ this old tunnel.
11. The builders covered the roof with ____________________ iron.
12. We don't have ____________________ food to feed everyone.
13. Some teachers were away so the classes were ____________________.
14. The fatal ____________________ occurred on the crossroads.
15. The car's ____________________ fumes made us nauseous.
16. The dispatched army decided to ____________________.

Parent/Teacher Signature   Date

Adding ion to base words

The suffix ion can be added to many words to form nouns.
Examples: reflect, reflection; express, expression

A The bracketed words below end in ct or ss. Make each end in ion to fit the meaning of the sentence.

1. This criminal has another ____________________ against him. (convict)
2. We asked the big children for ____________________ from the bullies. (protect)
3. Some of our rarest creatures are now faced with ____________________. (extinct)
4. The principal is going to make an ____________________ of our desks. (inspect)
5. We made a ____________________ of the books we wanted. (select)
6. The patient had a disastrous ____________________ to the drug. (react)
7. The ____________________ of form captains will be held soon. (elect)
8. I have an ____________________ to the way she is acting. (object)
9. His honesty and loyalty left a lasting ____________________ on me. (impress)
10. On Saturday morning a great ____________________ of floats came down the street. (process)
11. The pupil said he had a ____________________ to make. (confess)
12. This is my most loved ____________________ as my parents gave it to me. (possess)
13. She has a real ____________________ with being a star. (obsess)
14. What ____________________ will you enter when you leave school? (profess)
15. The ____________________ of the poor was terrible. (oppress)
16. Our class ____________________ about snakes was lively. (discuss)

B Make these words end in ion. Write each in a sentence.

1. inject ____
2. express ____

Parent/Teacher Signature　　　　　　　　Date

Adding ion or ation to base words

As with the word ending **ion**, the suffix **ation** can also be added to words to form nouns.
Examples: insert, insertion; indent, indentation

A Make each word in brackets below end in **ion** or **ation** so it fits the meaning of the sentence.

1. There was a ____________ ball for the graduating students. (present)
2. The blow made an ____________ in the soft metal. (indent)
3. He made a great ____________ at the meeting. (suggest)
4. There was a lot of traffic ____________ in the busy streets. (congest)
5. The ____________ of this disease is very important. (prevent)
6. They made a special ____________ for me. (except)
7. The ____________ of the city shocked the people. (invade)
8. A large ____________ took place in the old volcano. (erupt)
9. The ____________ of the newborn baby was approved by its parents. (adopt)
10. Much ____________ was put in the way of the hungry children. (tempt)
11. The ____________ of the book was very successful. (adapt)
12. A pine ____________ takes up a large area in the hills. (plant)
13. His powers of ____________ were legendary. (persuade)
14. A large ____________ of insects struck last year. (infest)
15. A serious ____________ broke out between the two gangs. (confront)
16. Her ____________ helped all humanity. (invent)

B Make these words end in **ion** or **ation**. Write each in a sentence.

1. distort ____________________________
2. lament ____________________________

Parent/Teacher Signature　　　　　　Date

Revision

A Make the words in the box end in **ion** and then write each in a sentence.

adopt	profess	collide	protect
explode	prevent	except	obsess
distinct	decide	process	erode

1. ______________________
2. ______________________
3. ______________________
4. ______________________
5. ______________________
6. ______________________
7. ______________________
8. ______________________
9. ______________________
10. ______________________
11. ______________________
12. ______________________

B Sort the words in the box under the headings below.

confession	location	rejection	dictation
operation	invention	agitation	exhaustion

+ ion (drop e)		+ ion (no change)	
________	________	________	________
________	________	________	________

Parent/Teacher Signature Date

Test

One word in each sentence is spelled wrongly.
Find that word and write it correctly on the line.

	Sentence	Answer
1	It is necessery to have proof of your age.	1
2	The men will escavate the deep hole.	2
3	A colision occurred at the corner last night.	3
4	Her writing is so bad it is ilegible.	4
5	There is a large pine plantashun nearby.	5
6	The teacher would not make any excheptions.	6
7	We had a discushun about her behaviour.	7
8	A large explodsion happened last night.	8
9	These buildings will only be a tempary measure.	9
10	The car has a punchure in the front tyre.	10
11	The teacher made an insepectsion of the room.	11
12	The distance of the seabirds' migrateion is amazing.	12

Total correct ________
12

Parent/Teacher Signature Date

UNIT 70

Vowel alternations

When you add suffixes to some words, the vowel sound changes from long to short.
Example: able (long a), ability (short a)

The words in the brackets below have a suffix added and contain the short vowel sound. Change them back to the base word containing the long vowel sound and write them in the spaces.

1. This company will ____________ a lot of cars this year. (production)
2. I hope to watch the next ____________ of my favourite program. (episodic)
3. The old fox was ____________ and cunning. (wisdom)
4. A long thin ____________ rose from the fire. (flammable)
5. She was convicted of the ____________ although she was innocent. (criminal)
6. Would you ____________ shut that door for me. (pleasant)
7. She made a ____________ error in not asking first. (gravity)
8. The teacher will ____________ the work today. (revision)
9. We explored the dark ____________. (cavity)
10. Michelle is the best ____________ in our grade. (athletic)
11. We will have to ____________ its future soon. (decision)
12. I do not ____________ if he did it. (knowledge)
13. We watched in awe as the ____________ erupted. (volcanic)
14. If we rub it hard it will ____________. (ignition)
15. She spent a lot of time studying ____________. (natural)
16. I ____________ you will not leave before we are finished. (assumption)

Write these words in sentences of your own:

humane ____

humanity ____

Parent/Teacher Signature   Date

UNIT 71

Change of meaning by stress

The words in the box change their meaning with a shift of stress in the word. These words are homographs, which have the same spellings but are pronounced differently. The underlined syllable is stressed. Write the correct words in the spaces below, underlining the stressed syllable.

(a) con/vict	**(c) ref/use**	**(e) des/ert**	**(g) con/tent**	**(i) min/ute**	**(k) ob/ject**
(b) con/vict	**(d) re/fuse**	**(f) des/ert**	**(h) con/tent**	**(j) mi/nute**	**(l) ob/ject**

1. We staggered across the dry, arid __________________.
2. I hope you won't __________________ me now that I need you.
3. We waited a whole __________________ for him to return.
4. This tiny morsel is __________________ compared with those large ones.
5. I __________________ strongly to your attitude in this matter.
6. The engraved cup was the only __________________ he desired.
7. The police want to __________________ him of the offence.
8. The __________________ was bound with chains.
9. I will certainly __________________ his invitation as I don't like him.
10. The __________________ was placed in the bin.
11. The __________________ of this book is very interesting.
12. I feel very __________________ now that I am finished.

Write these words in sentences of your own:

es/cort (a guard) ______________________________

es/cort (to accompany) ______________________________

in/valid (sick person) ______________________________

inval/id (not valid) ______________________________

Parent/Teacher Signature Date

Number prefixes

Prefixes are letters added to the beginning of a word.
Some prefixes denote a number.
Example: bi + cycle = bicycle (bi means two)

Each of the words in the box contains a number-related prefix. Write each beside its meaning below.

octopus	**centipede**	**polygon**	**semicircle**
monotonous	**millionaire**	**monarch**	**multitude**
unicycle	**unique**	**pentagon**	**semicolon**
decade	**bilingual**	**bisect**	**tripod**

1. an eight-tentacled sea creature ____________________
2. a small creature with 100 legs ____________________
3. a flat shape with many sides ____________________
4. half a circle shape ____________________
5. boring, focused on one thing ____________________
6. a person who is very, very wealthy ____________________
7. a ruler or king ____________________
8. a lot of people ____________________
9. a punctuation mark ____________________
10. a flat shape with five sides ____________________
11. a stand with three legs ____________________
12. to cut in half ____________________
13. only one of its kind ____________________
14. able to speak two languages ____________________
15. a cycle with one wheel ____________________
16. a period of ten years ____________________

Parent/Teacher Signature Date

Review

A Sort the words in the box that have come from Old English, Latin or Greek roots under their headings below.

trident	**beat**	**automatic**	**batter**
battle	**autobiography**	**bat**	**indent**
autograph	**dental**	**dentist**	**autonomy**

Old English root word	**Latin root word**	**Greek root word**
beatan (to strike)	dentis (tooth)	autos (self)
______________	______________	______________
______________	______________	______________
______________	______________	______________
______________	______________	______________

B Add **et**, **it**, **ar** or **or** to complete each word.

1. The burgl_____ was arrested by the police.
2. We filled the buck_____ with water.
3. The satellite will begin to orb_____ the Earth.
4. The worker is wearing a special helm_____.
5. The machine is connected to sol_____ power.
6. The dentist extracted the mol_____.
7. We welcomed the visit_____ to our school.
8. The inspector decided to aud_____ the accounts.

C Underline the words that contain a long vowel sound.

trust	cradle	attic	vacant
statue	beetle	lemon	lonely
hobby	stage	comma	nine

Parent/Teacher Signature Date

Test 1

Choose the correct spelling from the words in brackets and write it on the line.

1	The (burgler, burglar) was arrested by the police.	1
2	We showed the (visitor, visiter) where the office was.	2
3	There was a lot of (traffic, trafik) on the freeway.	3
4	Riley drank a whole (bottel, bottle) of water.	4
5	The apartment is presently (vacant, vacent).	5
6	Lily hopes to (acheave, achieve) all her goals.	6
7	The teacher gave a (lessen, lesson) about discrimination.	7
8	This farm has lots of (gooses, geese).	8
9	The (guest, guessed) was taken to her room.	9
10	I go to hockey (practice, practise) each evening.	10
11	The film star signed her (autograph, autograf).	11
12	The nurse tied a (bandage, bandige) over the wound.	12

Total correct ______ / 12

Parent/Teacher Signature   Date

Test 2

The underlined words are spelled incorrectly. Write each one correctly on the line.

	Sentence	Answer
1	He tried to signail us to stop.	1
2	The meat of a pig is baycon.	2
3	The bright lightening lit up the sky.	3
4	That sportsperson is very famus.	4
5	We have two pianoes at our school.	5
6	There are many different gasses in the atmosphere.	6
7	There are several monkies at the zoo.	7
8	The cows and their calfs are in the yard.	8
9	There were lots of mosquitos in the park.	9
10	We are not aloud to go on the excursion.	10
11	Our school tuckshop made a big prophet.	11
12	The wether has been hot lately.	12

Total correct ______ / 12

Parent/Teacher Signature Date

Test 3

One of the words in each of these sentences is spelled incorrectly. Circle the word and then write it correctly on the line.

1	We saw the dog in its kennal.	1
2	Barry tripped and injured his ankel.	2
3	A large tidil wave crashed on to the coast.	3
4	The soldier was awarded a meddel.	4
5	The smoke made it hard to breeth.	5
6	The racing cars roared around the cercut.	6
7	This town is a suberb of the city.	7
8	These are not artificial diamonds but are orthentic.	8
9	The cricketer dropt the catch.	9
10	A new house was builded in the street last year.	10
11	The mother cuddled her baby gentley.	11
12	The large processon of people was in the street.	12

Total correct ______
12

Parent/Teacher Signature Date

Useful Words

Students at this level should be aware of and be able to spell these words. These words should also be understood.

absence
accept
accident
according
adopt
affair
against
agreement
allege
already
annual
application
appreciate
argument
arrange
arrangement
arrive
article
assist
associate
association
assure
athletic
attention
automobile
avenue
beginning
believe
business
busy
career
celebration
century
certain
character
Christmas
circular
circumstance
citizen
colonies
combination
committee
common
complete
concern
condition
conference
consider
consideration
convenient
convention
cordially
course
decide
decision
develop
diamond
difference
different
difficulty
director
disappoint
discussion
distinguish
distribute
divide
doubt
drown
earliest
education
effect
elaborate
emergency
entertain
entitle
especially
estimate
evidence
examination
expense
experience
fascinate
February
finally
folks
foreign
further
general
government
guess
height
honour
illustrate
immediate
impossible
imprison
improvement
increase
injure
interest
investigate
invitation
issue
judgement
local
lose
machine
majority
manner
marriage
material
meant
mention
mere
minute
motion
national
necessary
neighbour
neither
object
occupy
official
often
opinion
organisation
organise
ought
particular
perhaps
piece
pleasant
political
popular
possible
practical
prefer
preliminary
prepare
principal
principle
probably
proceed
promise
provision
publication
purpose
really
receipt
receive
recent
recommend
refer
reference
relief
respectfully
responsible
salary
scene
search
secretary
secure
senate
separate
serious
service
session
sincerely
statement
stopped
success
suggest
summon
supply
system
testimony
theatre
their
therefore
together
tomorrow
too
total
towards
treasure
unfortunate
various
vessel
victim
visitor
volume
wear
Wednesday
weigh
whether
witness
wreck
written

WINK: Words I Need to Know

For many people, some words are often problematic to spell. Record words you are having difficulty with on this page.

Word	Word	Word

Some Tips for Learning to Spell

★ When you read, look out for the patterns of letters you find in words. Remembering these will help you spell words. For example, these words do not sound the same, but all contain a common letter pattern: cough, rough, through, thought, bough.

★ Take an interest in words, as this is useful in motivating you to persevere with improving your spelling ability.

★ Accept that some difficult words simply have to be learned. A useful strategy for this is the LOOK, COVER, WRITE, CHECK system.

LOOK at the word and try to form a pattern of the letters in your mind. Ensure you know the meaning of the word and how it is used.

COVER the word or remove it from your sight.

WRITE the word from memory.

CHECK if you are correct.

If wrong, begin the process again. If right, give yourself a pat on the back.

★ Learn to say words correctly. Many students often have spelling difficulties simply because they pronounce some words incorrectly, and spell them as they think they sound. For example: jumping, not jumpen.

★ Develop the dictionary habit. If you don't know how to spell a word, look it up. Did you know a dictionary is used more for finding the correct spelling of words rather than finding their meanings?

★ Become familiar with the more common rules and guides, and use them.

★ When you are writing and you have guessed the spelling of a word, always check it later.

★ Remember that incorrect spelling is easily noticed by others, so being a good speller can be an aid to employment.

Assessment

		T1	T2	T3	T4
★	Reads widely and takes an interest in words and their meanings.				
★	Is prepared to make informed attempts at spelling.				
★	Spells at a standard commensurate with his or her age.				
★	Uses a variety of methods to improve spelling skills, such as sounds and patterns.				
★	Takes care to review and proofread own writing attempts.				
★	Readily identifies errors in proofreading activities.				
★	Continually displays a determination and desire to improve spelling.				
★	Is aware that words that sound the same may have different spellings.				
★	Makes correct vowel alternation from long to short vowels.				

Comments

Teacher

____

____

Student

____

____

Glossary of Terms

adjective
A word that describes nouns or other words.
Examples: **gold** (noun), **golden** (adjective)
wool (noun), **woollen** (adjective)

anagram
A *word* or words that contains exactly the same letters but in a different order.
Examples: **pea**, **ape**; **fowl**, **flow**, **wolf**;
seaside, **disease**

assimilation
Refers to absorbed or assimilated prefixes, when the spelling and sound of the consonant in a prefix has been absorbed into the spelling and sound at the beginning of the *root word* to which the prefix is added. Examples: **ad** + **cumulo** (I make into a heap) = **accumulate;**
come + **ligo** (I join or unite with) = **college**

base word
A *word* to which *prefixes* and *suffixes* can be added. Example: **obey** (base word) + **dis** (prefix) = **disobey** + **ed** (suffix) = **disobeyed**

comparative
An *adjective* that shows a degree of comparison between two or more things.
Examples: **big** (one), **bigger** (two), **biggest** (three or more); Jack is tall but Tom is taller.

complex consonant group
A consonant unit (**ch**, **ck**, **dge**, **tch**) occurring at the end of a *word*, determined by the preceding *vowel* sound. Examples: **tch** follows a short vowel sound, as in **catch**, **fetch**, **itch**, **crutch**;
ch follows a long vowel sound, as in **beach** and **coach**

compound word
A *word* made up of two or more smaller words, often developing first as a hyphenated word.
Examples: **butter** + **fly** = **butterfly**;
gold field, gold-field, goldfield

consonant
A letter in which the air is in some way impeded when pronounced. There are 21 consonants in the alphabet, all the letters that are not *vowels*.

consonant alternation
The process in which the pronunciation of different words derived from the same source changes in the base word. Examples: **sign** to **signal** (silent **g** changes to hard **g**);
music to **musician** (**k** changes to **sh** sound)

consonant blend
When two or more *consonants* come together to blend a sound. Examples: **stick**, **sky**, **brown**, **straw**. Consonant blends may be initial blends (**frog**), medial (middle) blends (**blister**), or final blends (**stamp**).

contraction
A *word* in which one or more letters have been omitted and in their place an apostrophe inserted.
Examples: **I would** becomes **I'd**;
is not becomes **isn't**

digraph
A combination of letters that represents a single sound. There are *consonant* digraphs and *vowel* digraphs. Common consonant digraphs include **sh**, **ch**, **th** and **wh**. (Consonant digraphs at the beginning of a word are called an onset.) A vowel digraph is called a *diphthong*.

diphthong
Two *vowel* sounds that glide together to make a single unit of sound.
Examples: the **oy** in **toy** and the **ou** in **cloud**

eponym
A *word* that has come from the names of a person or place. Example: The word **bantam**, meaning a small foul, comes from a place in Indonesia called Bantam, in Taro.

etymology
The study of the origin and historical development of words.

homograph
A *word* that is spelled the same as another word, but each word is pronounced differently and has a different meaning (a type of *homonym*).
Examples: **desert** (dry barren area) and **desert** (abandon); **close** (near) and **close** (shut)

homonym
A *word* that is spelled and/or pronounced the same as another word but each word has a different meaning. *Homographs* and *homophones* are both types of homonym, and some homonyms are both homographs and homophones. Examples: **tear** (rip) and **tear** (result of crying)**; fair** (blond) and **fare** (cost of a train ticket)**; bank** (place to exchange money) and **bank** (either side of a river)

homophone
A *word* that is pronounced the same as another word, but each word has a different spelling and a different meaning.
Examples: **bear** (a furry animal) and **bare** (naked);
sure (certain) and **shore** (coastline)

letter pattern
A letter sequence that functions as a unit and is related to a consistent category of sound.
Example: **one** = **bone**, **cone**, **tone**

long vowel
The sound of a *vowel* (**a**, **e**, **i**, **o**, **u**) that says its letter name, or is an *r-influenced vowel.*
Examples: **same**, **bacon**, **far**, **concrete**, **fever**, **fine**, **rival**, **fir**, **cone**, **robot**, **core**, **cute**, **student**, **purr**

noun
A *word* that refers to the names of everything around us.

phonics
The systematic relationship between letters and sounds.

phonogram
One of a group of words that end in a common rhyme and that vary only in the beginning *consonant.*
Examples: **back**, **hack**, **lack**, **sack**, **tack**

plural
More than one. Most words make their plurals by adding an **s**. However, there are other ways to make the plurals of words.
Examples: **girl**, **girls**; **watch**, **watches**; **city**, **cities**; **piano**, **pianos**; **knife**, **knives**; **tooth**, **teeth**; **mouse**, **mice**

portmanteau word
A word created by joining a part of one word to a part of another. They were first created by Lewis Carroll, who wrote Alice in Wonderland.
Examples: **brunch** from breakfast and lunch; **smog** from smoke and fog

possessive
A *word* form that shows ownership or possession by adding an apostrophe before an **s** (**'s**) to singular nouns and adding an apostrophe after the *plural* ending for plural nouns.
Examples: one boy**'s** bike, three boy**s'** bikes (but five child**ren's** toys)

prefix
Letters added to the beginning of a word, sometimes to make its opposite. We simply add these and no spelling changes to the base word are necessary.
Example: **in** + **visible** = **invisible**

r-influenced vowel
A vowel sound that is determined by the letter **r** following it. Example: the **a** in **far** is a *long vowel* sound but the **a** in **fad** is a *short vowel* sound.

root word
A *word* or word part that has its origin in Old English, Latin or Greek and that provides the basis of many other words.
Example: **aero** (air) = **aerial**, **aeroplane**, **aerobics**

schwa
A vowel sound that often occurs in an unstressed *syllable.*
Example: the uh sound in the first syllable of the word **above**

short vowel
The sound of a *vowel* (**a**, **e**, **i**, **o** and **u**) that is clipped — a short sound. It is sometimes said short vowel sounds are the "baby" sounds.
Examples: **bat**, **bet**, **bit**, **bottle**, **but**

shortened word
A word that, over the years, has become shortened.
Example: **omnibus** (full version in use fifty or more years ago), **bus** (current usage)

silent (unsounded) letter
A letter in some words that is not pronounced but is still included in the word.
Examples: **lamb**, **know**, **pneumonia**, **sword**, **wrap**

suffix
A *word* ending that alters the word's part of speech (noun to adjective, for example) or meaning. Spelling changes are often needed.
Example: **beauty** + **ful** = **beautiful**

syllable
A sound unit that includes only one sounded *vowel.* The vowel may be preceded or followed by several *consonants.* Words can be divided into their syllables. This is a useful spelling technique.
Example: **development** = **de** / **vel** / **op** / **ment**

tense
A word form that shows when an event is happening. Words that change from present to past or future tense often change their spelling in some way. Sometimes the word itself changes or a helping verb is added.
Examples: Today I **play** (present). Yesterday I **played** (past). Tomorrow I will **play** (future);
Today I **freeze** (present). Yesterday I **froze** (past).
Next week I will be **freezing** (future).

vowel
A letter in which the air passes through the mouth without obstruction when pronounced. The letters **a**, **e**, **i**, **o** and **u** are vowels. Note: **y** does the work of the vowels **i** and **e** in words such as **cry** (long **i**), **mystery** (short **i**) and **weary** (long **e**).

vowel alternation
The process by which the pronunciation of a *vowel* changes in the base word while the spelling does not change.
Example: the long-to-short vowel change in the related words **crime** and **criminal**

word
A unit of meaning. A word may be a simple *syllable* or a combination of syllables. A word may contain smaller units of meaning within it.

Answers, Class 6

Unit 1

A

1. accident
2. bandage
3. candle
4. attic
5. avenue
6. tragic
7. canvas
8. address
9. package
10. baptise

B

Short a sound: cattle, capsule, maggot

Long a sound: agent, sacred, painter

Unit 2

A

1. decay
2. raven
3. raisin
4. baseball
5. crayon
6. bacon
7. nation
8. pavement
9. cradle
10. mistake
11. subway
12. vacant

B

Short a sound: hammer, traffic, pattern, gallop, napkin, plastic

Long a sound: dismay, debate, basement, grateful, waiter, vapour

Unit 3

A

1. beetle
2. compete
3. beaver
4. cheetah
5. fever
6. steeple
7. delete
8. canteen
9. eager
10. conceal

B

Short e sound: metal, denim, lemon, pedal, credit, feather

Long e sound: trapeze, free, breezy, agree, repeat, appeal, breathe

Unit 4

A

1. spider
2. bridle
3. nightmare
4. polite
5. rival
6. iceberg
7. sinus
8. lightning
9. reptile
10. sightseer
11. frighten
12. quiet

B

Short i sound: skinny, ribbon, river, picture, blizzard, signal

Long i sound: describe, wildlife, minus, visor, siren, ninety

Unit 5

A

1. explode
2. postage
3. robot
4. lonely
5. telescope
6. propose
7. violent
8. broken
9. donate
10. enclose

B

Short o sound: comet, bottle, nozzle, hobby, monster, comma

Long o sound: alone, snowfall, almost, local, mower, token

Unit 6

A

1. rescue
2. tune
3. pupil
4. avenue
5. refute
6. puncture
7. bugle
8. population
9. furniture
10. value
11. cure
12. future

B

Short u sound: custard, product, mustard, lumping, plum, crust

Long u sound: rescue, statue, avenue, introduce, confuse, perfume

Unit 7 Revision

1. accident
2. bacon
3. daisy
4. cradle
5. waiter
6. pony
7. postage
8. lightning
9. hobby
10. violent
11. minus
12. beaver
13. compete
14. cure
15. tragic
16. baptise

Unit 8 Test 1

1. lonely
2. chosen
3. iceberg
4. reptile
5. delight
6. famous
7. maintain
8. attic
9. mammals
10. cheetah
11. fever
12. canteen

Unit 9 Test 2

1. ignite
2. frozen
3. cradle
4. traffic
5. donate
6. explode
7. spider
8. bugle
9. shampoo
10. puncture
11. address
12. furniture

Unit 10

1. torpedoes
2. pianos
3. pages
4. trees
5. bushes
6. shampoos
7. foxes
8. rodeos
9. grottoes
10. gases
11. chairs
12. churches
13. mangos
14. guesses
15. radios
16. plates

Unit 11

1. crays
2. cries
3. donkeys
4. journeys
5. duties
6. storeys
7. territories
8. parties
9. delicacies
10. trays
11. monkeys
12. medleys
13. subways
14. tallies
15. dictionaries
16. buggies

Unit 12

1. reefs
2. hooves
3. lives
4. carafes
5. shelves
6. beliefs
7. wharves

8. wives
9. roofs
10. leaves
11. calves
12. cuffs
13. cliffs
14. elves
15. giraffes
16. chiefs

Unit 13
1. teeth
2. scissors
3. feet
4. geese
5. pliers
6. larvae
7. children
8. trousers
9. spectacles
10. radii
11. applause
12. lice
13. cattle
14. fungi
15. trout
16. women

Unit 14 Revision
A
1. fly, flies
2. berry, berries
3. diary, diaries
4. photo, photos
5. flood, floods
6. glass glasses
7. story, stories
8. atlas, atlases
9. sky, skies
10. patch, patches
11. trolley, trolleys
12. wolf, wolves
13. monkey, monkeys

B
1. thieves
2. foxes
3. geese
4. shampoos
5. deer
6. branches
7. diaries
8. mosquitoes
9. loaves
10. trolleys

Unit 15 Test
1. buses
2. stories
3. monkeys
4. wolves
5. guesses
6. giraffes
7. leaves
8. volcanoes
9. kangaroos
10. photos
11. oceans
12. foxes

Unit 16
1. ceiling
2. cellar
3. practise
4. prophet
5. profit
6. lessen
7. presents
8. council
9. presence
10. sealing
11. practice
12. allowed
13. lesson
14. counsel
15. seller
16. aloud

Unit 17
1. mussel
2. stationery
3. whether
4. farther
5. missed
6. mayor
7. mourning
8. patience
9. mist
10. muscle
11. stationary
12. weather
13. father
14. mare
15. morning
16. patients

Unit 18
1. wegan: wagon, wag
2. sceran: scrape, sharp
3. beatan: battle, beat
4. faran: ferry, fare
5. witan: wisdom, wise
6. grafan: engrave, groove
7. bindan: bandage, bondage
8. stede: homestead, instead
9. foda: fodder, feed
10. dragan: dray, draught

Unit 19
A
1. apple
2. kennel
3. eagle
4. camel
5. beetle
6. ankle
7. bugle
8. parcel
9. bottle
10. shovel
11. novel

B
1. bicycle
2. kettle
3. gravel
4. jungle
5. tunnel
6. barrel
7. squirrel
8. quarrel
9. needle
10. turtle

Unit 20
A
1. pedal
2. petal
3. lentil
4. nostril
5. peril
6. gerbil
7. pencil
8. sandal
9. crystal
10. fossil
11. final
12. mammal

B
1. cordial
2. council
3. tidal
4. tonsils
5. feral
6. metal
7. central
8. peril
9. medal
10. evil

Unit 21
A
1. core
2. door
3. sponsor
4. roar
5. meteor
6. broad
7. four
8. floor
9. enormous
10. moor

B
1. loaves
2. approach
3. moat
4. coach
5. throat
6. coax
7. cocoa
8. hoax

Unit 22
A
1. peace
2. conceal
3. bleach
4. breathe
5. increased
6. eagle
7. decrease
8. dreary
9. disease
10. grease

B
Long e sound: grease, least, increase
Short e sound: head, spread, weather
Long a sound: break, steak, great

Unit 23
A
1. circus
2. chirp
3. circle
4. smirk
5. thirty
6. birth
7. dirty
8. circuit
9. thirsty
10. stirring

B

1. turtle
2. purple
3. hurdle
4. surgeon
5. suburb
6. turnip
7. turkey
8. surfer

Unit 24

A

1. nausea
2. gauze
3. auction
4. autumn
5. tarpaulin
6. sausage
7. automatic
8. cauliflower
9. authentic
10. exhaust

B

1. moustache
2. flounder
3. cougar
4. toucan
5. acoustics
6. mountain
7. routine
8. soup
9. cousin
10. amount

Unit 25 Revision

A

au = or sound: authentic, exhaust

au = short o sound: cauliflower, auction

ou = short u sound: cousin, rough

ou = long oo sound: soup, troupe

ou = ow sound: hound, flounder

oa = long o sound: coast, loaves

B

1. circus
2. coach
3. auction
4. routine
5. flounder
6. squirrel
7. crystal
8. anchor
9. surgeon
10. inventor

Unit 26 Test 1

1. circle
2. autumn
3. moustache
4. cauliflower
5. ankle
6. bicycle
7. sandals
8. council
9. fossils
10. sponsor
11. surgeon
12. spread

Unit 27 Test 2

1. exhaust
2. soup
3. disease
4. weather
5. petal
6. cordial
7. bugle
8. mammal
9. mayor
10. treaty
11. circuit
12. final

Unit 28

A

1. melted
2. dozed
3. scrubbed
4. dropped
5. caught
6. froze
7. built
8. taught
9. knelt
10. left

B

1. baked
2. jumped
3. climbed
4. hopped
5. clapped
6. chose
7. forgot
8. hid
9. gave
10. tore
11. wrote
12. swore

Unit 29

1. the cowboy's saddles
2. the chair's legs
3. the bicycle's handlebars
4. the book's pages
5. the lady's bags
6. the ladies' bags
7. the children's toys
8. the women's homes
9. the diaries' pages
10. the police officer's cap
11. the geese's feathers
12. the butterflies' wings
13. the butterfly's antenna
14. the men's glasses

Unit 30

1. proudly
2. wearily
3. easily
4. sweetly
5. truly
6. gently
7. noisily
8. carefully
9. annually
10. hopefully
11. hungrily
12. terribly
13. clumsily
14. angrily
15. quickly
16. comfortably

Unit 31

1. selection
2. reaction
3. decoration
4. imitation
5. extinction
6. profession
7. creation
8. fascination
9. procession
10. affection
11. prediction
12. aversion

Unit 32 Revision

A

1. the cat's claws
2. the child's toys
3. the birds' nests
4. the books' covers
5. the ladies' glasses
6. the women's dresses
7. the trees' leaves
8. the giraffe's neck

B

1. easily
2. noisily
3. luckily
4. drowsily
5. gently
6. idly
7. possibly
8. probably

C

1. swam
2. crept
3. drank
4. felt
5. bought
6. rang
7. rose
8. knew
9. wrote
10. left

Unit 33 Test

1. chopped
2. taught
3. froze
4. ladies'
5. butterfly's
6. greedily
7. angrily
8. truly
9. gently
10. dropped
11. children's
12. child's

Unit 34

1. permit (v)
2. record (n)
3. desert (n)
4. record (v)
5. rebel (v)
6. subject (v)
7. subject (n)
8. combat (v)
9. combat (n)
10. permit (n)
11. desert (v)
12. rebel (n)

Unit 35

A

1. it is
2. did not
3. we have
4. I am
5. we are
6. that is
7. you are
8. what is

B

1. she's
2. I've
3. there's
4. they'll
5. don't
6. you'd
7. they're
8. would've

Unit 36

1. missile
2. current
3. conductor
4. operate
5. factory
6. proprietor
7. signature
8. abbreviate
9. dentist
10. actor
11. fortress
12. culprit

Unit 37

1. bucket
2. profit
3. summit
4. trumpet
5. wallet
6. hermit
7. blanket
8. scarlet
9. audit
10. merit
11. orbit
12. budget
13. gadget
14. helmet
15. tablet
16. vomit

Unit 38

1. hangar
2. meteor
3. scissors
4. tutor
5. solar
6. razor
7. molar
8. cellar
9. editor
10. beggar
11. mayor
12. cougar
13. visitor
14. cedar
15. nectar
16. cursor

Unit 39

A

1. comb
2. hour
3. yolk
4. beret
5. scent
6. gnat

B

1. scissors (c)
2. scheme (h)
3. wren (w)
4. depot (t)
5. sword (w)
6. wreck (w)
7. dinghy (h)
8. tomb (b)
9. wrist (w)
10. guard (u)

C

1. science (c)
2. thumb (b)
3. knives (k)
4. hymn (n)
5. honest (h)
6. aisle (s)
7. sword (w)
8. answer (w)
9. wreath (w)
10. handsome (d)

Unit 40

1. aphids
2. rough
3. nephew
4. sphere
5. cough
6. laughter
7. dolphin
8. graph
9. enough
10. tough
11. photograph
12. pharmacy

Unit 41

1. scratch
2. hedge
3. barge
4. badge
5. rich
6. sketch
7. gauge
8. smudge
9. budge
10. sandwich
11. judge
12. strange
13. ditch
14. clutch
15. dodge
16. grudge

Unit 42

A

1. concluded
2. dangerous
3. necessary
4. astonish
5. crocodile
6. rectangle
7. calendar
8. octopus
9. numerous
10. continue
11. adventure
12. lemonade
13. museum
14. vacation
15. underwear
16. potato

B

1. or / din / ar / y
2. fol / low / ing
3. choc / o / late
4. pos / ses / sive

Unit 43 Revision

A

1. basket
2. profit
3. cheddar
4. sugar
5. razor
6. hatchet
7. exit
8. faucet
9. traitor
10. lunar

B

1. wren
2. tomb
3. handsome
4. island
5. knife
6. scheme
7. gnat
8. yolk
9. scent
10. autumn

C

1. tel / e / phone
2. rap / id / ly
3. el / e / phant
4. sec / ure / ly
5. in / ter / view
6. fur / nit / ure
7. ker / o / sene
8. in / dig / nant
9. cir / cu / late
10. con / tes / ted

Unit 44 Test 1

1. orbit
2. gadget
3. wallet
4. bandit
5. visitor
6. solar
7. editor
8. nephew
9. pharmacy
10. sketch
11. scissors
12. guard

Unit 45 Test 2

1. judge
2. dinghy
3. profit
4. cougar
5. basket
6. stretch
7. clutch
8. tablet
9. wrist
10. answer
11. dolphin
12. laughter

Unit 46

1. hopped
2. switched
3. chased
4. painted
5. occurred
6. saved
7. tasted
8. gripped

9. excelled
10. referred
11. orbited
12. adjusted
13. submitted
14. changed
15. begged
16. lasted

Unit 47
1. chopping
2. switching
3. sitting
4. lecturing
5. occurring
6. clapping
7. dancing
8. catching
9. excelling
10. referring
11. orbiting
12. limiting
13. submitting
14. advising
15. exploding
16. blaming

Unit 48
1. explosion
2. imitation
3. donation
4. pollution
5. decoration
6. location
7. operation
8. circulation
9. creation
10. translation
11. decision
12. graduation
13. collision
14. illustration
15. erosion
16. vibration

Unit 49
1. vigilant
2. reluctance
3. fragrance
4. instant
5. tolerant
6. defiance
7. malignant
8. relevance
9. petulant
10. brilliance
11. elegant
12. exuberance
13. resistant
14. extravagance
15. significance
16. observant

Unit 50 Revision

A

+ ed (no change): painted, played, crawled, helped, lasted, weeded
+ ed (double last letter): dropped, skipped, travelled, chopped, clapped, hopped

B

+ ing (drop final e): hoping, writing, using, driving
+ ing (no change): crawling, washing, pushing, sleeping
+ ing (double last letter): spotting, travelling, occurring, swimming

C

+ ant: vigilant, petulant, malignant, elegant
+ ion: decoration, location, migration, translation

Unit 51 Test
1. hopped
2. chasing
3. occurred
4. advising
5. exploding
6. pollution
7. circulation
8. resistant
9. vigilant
10. extravagant
11. petulant
12. resistance

Unit 52

A
1. butterfly
2. suitcase
3. pancake
4. overcoat
5. signpost
6. sunset
7. everywhere
8. toothache
9. hamburger
10. towtruck

B
1. football
2. toothbrush or hairbrush
3. handcuffs
4. armchair
5. shinbone
6. skindiver
7. eyebrow
8. fingernail

C
1. earthquake
2. seahorse
3. notebook
4. skateboard
5. sunburn
6. signpost
7. moonlight
8. hayfever

UINT 53
1. procession
2. ability
3. natural
4. inspiration
5. resignation
6. president
7. admiration
8. conduction
9. reduction
10. production
11. composition
12. deprivation
13. decision
14. resident
15. relation
16. division

Unit 54

A
1. autograph
2. calligraphy
3. asterisk
4. biologist
5. monopoly
6. democracy
7. metre
8. dynamite
9. electric
10. geology

B
1. telescope
2. bicycle
3. alphabet
4. automatic
5. monopoly

C
1. astronomer
2. photograph
3. television
4. microscope

Unit 55
1. gadget ✓
2. genius ×
3. genie ×
4. goggles ✓
5. gutter ✓
6. gully ✓
7. gyrate ×
8. general ×
9. gesture ×
10. gossip ✓
11. guitar ✓
12. gypsy ×
13. gorilla ✓
14. guilty ✓
15. giraffe ×
16. giant ×

Unit 56
1. cider ×
2. camel ✓
3. cereal ×
4. culprit ✓
5. counterfeit ✓
6. cement ×
7. candidate ✓
8. circular ×
9. census ×
10. campus ✓
11. camouflage ✓
12. citizen ×
13. certain ×
14. cockatoo ✓
15. circus ×
16. coffee ✓

Unit 57

A
1. moist
2. voice
3. avoid
4. disappoint
5. joint
6. loiter
7. poisonous
8. appoint

B
1. receipt
2. neigh
3. neither
4. vein
5. weight
6. sleigh

7. seize
8. deceive
9. conceited
10. ceiling

Unit 58
1. village
2. voyage
3. pigeon
4. dungeon
5. sausage
6. fragile
7. courage
8. legend
9. angel
10. savage
11. margin
12. gorgeous
13. engine
14. carriage
15. storage
16. budget

Unit 59
1. preserve
2. liberty
3. surround
4. thirsty
5. certain
6. turkey
7. rhinoceros
8. encountered
9. reverse
10. interrupt
11. desert
12. cutlery
13. vermin
14. interfere
15. survive
16. surprise

Unit 60
1. python
2. reply
3. rhyming
4. amplify
5. magnify
6. cyclone
7. hyphen
8. nylon
9. hydrant
10. beautify
11. bypass
12. tyrant
13. hygiene
14. cycle
15. defy
16. stylish

Unit 61 Revision
A
Hard g sound: guitar, goggles, guilty, gossip
Soft g sound: gypsy, giraffe, genius, giant
B
Hard c sound: cockatoo, cactus, coffee, camoflauge
Soft c sound: cider, cement, citizen, cereal
C
Long a sound: weight, sleigh, eighty, neigh
Long e sound: receipt, seize, deceive, ceiling

Unit 62 Test 1
1. genius
2. certain
3. cockatoo
4. census
5. seize
6. vein
7. sausage
8. legends
9. interfere
10. thirsty
11. python
12. hydrant

Unit 63 Test 2
1. bicycle
2. stylish
3. turkey
4. cutlery
5. surprise
6. voyage
7. appoint
8. disappoint
9. voice
10. cereal
11. genius
12. guitar
13. survive
14. general
15. citizen
16. receipt

Unit 64
1. customary
2. secretary
3. vocabulary
4. elementary
5. necessary
6. stationary
7. burglary
8. salary
9. revolutionary
10. boundary
11. diary
12. anniversary
13. documentary
14. temporary
15. imaginary
16. solitary

Unit 65
1. subscription
2. adjective
3. obstinate
4. attention
5. disregarded
6. difficult
7. illegible
8. impartial
9. immature
10. excavate
11. corrugated
12. sufficient
13. combined
14. collision
15. exhaust
16. surrender

Unit 66
A
1. conviction
2. protection
3. extinction
4. inspection
5. selection
6. reaction
7. election
8. objection
9. impression
10. procession
11. confession
12. possession
13. obsession
14. profession
15. oppression
16. discussion
B
1. injection
2. expression

Unit 67
A
1. presentation
2. indentation
3. suggestion
4. congestion
5. prevention
6. exception
7. invasion
8. eruption
9. adoption
10. temptation
11. adaptation
12. plantation
13. persuasion
14. infestation
15. confrontation
16. invention
B
1. distortion
2. lamentation

Unit 68 Revision
A
1. adoption
2. explosion
3. distinction
4. profession
5. prevention
6. decision
7. collision
8. exception
9. procession
10. protection
11. obsession
12. erosion
B
+ ion (drop e): operation, location, agitation, dictation
+ ion (no change): confession, invention, rejection, exhaustion

Unit 69 Test
1. necessary
2. excavate
3. collision
4. illegible
5. plantation
6. exceptions
7. discussion
8. explosion
9. temporary
10. puncture
11. inspection
12. migration

Unit 70
1. produce
2. episode
3. wise
4. flame
5. crime
6. please
7. grave
8. revise
9. cave
10. athlete
11. decide
12. know
13. volcano
14. ignite
15. nature
16. assume

Unit 71
1. des/ert
2. des/ert
3. min/ute
4. mi/nute
5. ob/ject
6. ob/ject
7. con/vict
8. con/vict
9. re/fuse
10. ref/use
11. con/tent
12. con/tent

Unit 72
1. octopus
2. centipede
3. polygon
4. semicircle
5. monotonous
6. millionaire
7. monarch
8. multitude
9. semicolon
10. pentagon
11. tripod
12. bisect
13. unique
14. bilingual
15. unicycle
16. decade

Unit 73 Review

A

Old English roots
beatan (to strike): battle, beat, bat, batter

Latin roots
dentis (tooth): trident, dental, dentist, indent

Greek roots
autos (self): autograph, autobiography, automatic, autonomy

B
1. burglar
2. bucket
3. orbit
4. helmet
5. solar
6. molar
7. visitor
8. audit

C

statue
cradle
beetle
stage
vacant
lonely
nine

Unit 74 Test 1
1. burglar
2. visitor
3. traffic
4. bottle
5. vacant
6. achieve
7. lesson
8. geese
9. guest
10. practice
11. autograph
12. bandage

Unit 75 Test 2
1. signal
2. bacon
3. lightning
4. famous
5. pianos
6. gases
7. monkeys
8. calves
9. mosquitoes
10. allowed
11. profit
12. weather

Unit 76 Test 3
1. kennel
2. ankle
3. tidal
4. medal
5. breathe
6. circuit
7. suburb
8. authentic
9. dropped
10. built
11. gently
12. procession